The Ele

The gap between expect.　　.... reality is where many couples experience disagreement and discouragement. With the help of Dr. Karampatsos, and the examples of other couples, you will learn to bridge that gap and experience a healthy, whole marriage. If you are looking for hope and help, read this book!

-Rod Loy
Author of *Three Questions, Immediate Obedience,* and
After the Honeymoon

Full of practical advice, *The Elephant in the Marriage*, takes a theological and psychological approach to create a thriving marriage. Dr. Karampatsos equips couples with excellent strategies to establish a healthier relationship while showing them how to overcome destructive cycles. I believe this book is a must-read for couples looking to transform their marriages in a meaningful and life-changing way.

-Wilfredo "Choco" De Jesus
Lead Pastor, New Life Covenant Church
Author of *Move into More, Stay the Course, In the Gap*
and *Amazing Faith*

The Elephant in the Marriage is a treatise that carefully considers the theological, scientific, cultural, gender–unique, and psychological perspectives on marriage. Dr. Karampatsos provides a much-needed challenge to all of us to think beyond our own experience of the marriage dynamic and place a greater emphasis upon the experience of our spouse.

-Erik Sundquist, LCSW-C
National Director, Safe Harbor Christian Counseling

The Elephant in the Marriage offers married couples, from a Christian perspective, both theoretical and practical help to allow them to fulfill their goals for healthy relationships. Jason Karampatsos, Ph.D., has the insight to offer this help, based on his perspective as a licensed professional counselor, ordained minister, husband and father. He draws on the wisdom of great thinkers ranging from Plato to Carl Rogers. This book is a "must read" for newlyweds as well as those who have been married for many decades.

-Anne Marie "Nancy" Wheeler, J.D.
Licensed Attorney, Risk Management Consultant for the ACA, and Co-Author of *The Counselor and the Law*

Rarely does a book come along that makes a real and lasting impact in the lives of its readers. This is just what Dr. Jason accomplishes in his book, *The Elephant in the Marriage*. Many popular marriage and relationship-building books offer some good tips and inspiration, but in time, it seems that the advice becomes 'old techniques'. *The Elephant in the Marriage* however deals with lasting principles of marital relationships, and when applied, undoubtedly the reader will encounter real tools to experience profound and permanent change.

–Bill McDonald
Missionary, Author, Founder of Unsión Television Network

This book is a must read for anyone longing for improvement in their marriage relationship—and that ought to be all of us. Backed by years of counseling expertise, Dr. Jason Karampatsos is a trustworthy source for helping to make your marriage and mine all that God longs for it to be. Although this book offers great information, the hope held out for all readers is transformation.

-Marilyn N. Anderes
Author of *More* and *From the Heart of the Word*

From the moment I read the introduction of Dr. Karampatsos' book, I knew there was here a great resource for anyone concerned about healthy marriages. His practical insights are applicable for couples who are in their first or fiftieth year of marriage. I also loved the quotes and practical applications he has interwoven throughout the book. Whether it is for personal use or for a valued leadership tool, I highly commend this book to you.

-Don Meyer, Ph.D.
President, University of Valley Forge

Marriage is the most important relationship we commit to here on earth. There are many resources to pick from when it comes to focusing on a great marriage. But in the plethora of marriage resources, Jason's perspective and expertise is one of the best. If you want a healthy marriage, you need to read this book. If you are struggling in your marriage, you need to read this book. If you are going to get married, you need to read this book. If you want your happily ever after, you need to read this book.

-Trinity Jordan
Author of *Sabotage: How Insecurity Destroys Everything*

Dr. Jason Karampatsos brings a wealth of personal study, research, and experience to the discussion of how to help Christian marriages transition from survival mode to vibrant relationships which reflect the grace and blessing of God. Jason has applied his skill as a counselor with great success helping couples within our network of over one thousand credentialed ministers. I am confident his insights will provide practical tools for those committed to producing healthy marriages in a challenging world.

-Ken Burtram
Superintendent, Potomac Ministry Network

The Elephant in the Marriage

in the

Discover What is Trampling Your Marital Satisfaction
and How to Enjoy a Thriving Marriage

Jason M Karampatsos, PhD

Cover artwork provided by Adobe Stock:
#122550846 & #104194114
All other artwork and photography © 2019 Jason Karampatsos, PhD
Edited by Jill Miklosovic, Annapolis, Maryland

Note: In most of the stories in this book, the names and details have
been changed to protect anonymity.

ISBN:
ISBN-13: 9781794442788

To my greatest fan, friend and cheerleader, who has encouraged me, spoken truth to me, and prayed for me while the rest of the world was still sleeping. Thank you for seeing the impact we can have for the Gospel by strengthening marriages, and your unwavering commitment to begin at home with ours.

Jennifer, *this book is for you.*
.

CONTENTS

ACKNOWLEDGMENTS

There are so many people who have come alongside me during the journey of taking this book from just an idea to what you now hold in your hands. The Lord has been so gracious and has blessed me beyond what I deserve or could have ever imagined. I could never have done all that He has open doors for me to do without His love, grace, mercy, and some truly precious people He has used to truly enrich my time here on earth.

First of all, my best friend, soul mate, ministry partner, the mother of three of God's greatest gifts in my life, and my wife. Jennifer, I am the man I am today because of your love for me and your love for the Lord. I am just one of countless individuals you have impacted for eternity with your infectious smile and never-yielding zeal for God. You continue to see the good in me, often even before it is reality.

I also want to thank…

Autumn, Hailey, and Christian. You sacrificed countless hours so that this book could bless others, and you continue to do so each and every week as pastor's kids. Your love, support, and encouragement mean more than you will possibly ever know. (If you are reading this, I have my end of a promise to now hold up!)

My editor Jill Miklosovic. You helped shape the words of this book more than any other while maintaining the voice God had for it. Thank you for your commitment and investment of time and talent.

My long-time agent, now retired, Leslie Stobbe. Although we were not able to get this to print before you retired, you tirelessly knocked on doors for a book you believed could make a difference. Thank you for believing in me and for your guidance and encouragement.

My church family at Cornerstone who helped support me while I was writing and editing this book, and my church family at New Life who have shared me as God continues to open doors to impact lives and marriages.

Brian Griswold, co-founder of *The City of Refuge Counseling Network*. Who would have thought when we first met in graduate school that God would have hitched us together to touch generations of families by impacting pastors, missionaries, and evangelists find health and thriving relationships with God, families, and others?

My trusted friend and accountability partner, John Dingle. You have stood by me, cheered me on, encouraged me by your bold faith for almost half of my time here on this planet. No matter where God moves us, I have been grateful that we have remained best of friends.

Pastor, author, and Circle Maker, Mark Batterson. Your gift of *The Circle Maker* was my first inspiration to write. I am grateful for your generosity of time over the years; opening your office up to me and helping me change a truly awful title for one that is much better. Thank you for encouraging me to "not bury the lead" and for some practical advice. I was learning even if you didn't know how much you were teaching me.

The hundreds of couples over the years who have been a part of our Marriage 101, Marriage 201, and Thriving Marriage classes. You have helped Jennifer and I hone the message that God ultimately wanted to make it into this book, as well as giving us real-time feedback of what clearly should not.

FOREWORD

Why do marriages fail? And why is it that so many couples can't seem to get beyond the barriers that hold them back from having a marriage that thrives instead of merely settling for surviving? ***The Elephant in the Marriage*** is more than a book about marriage, it is a marriage GPS. If you will implement the truths shared in these pages, it can lead you from your current marriage reality, to what God has always wanted it to be.

Knowing Dr Jason for several years, and seeing first hand couples that have been transformed by his wisdom and insight, gives me hope that it can be repeated countless times in marriages everywhere. The reason I believe in what is found in the following pages, is the heart behind them. In the years I have observed and served with Dr Jason Karampatsos, the passion that he has for walking with people though difficult and challenging places in their lives is what drives him. He truly loves people enough to speak the truth to them in a practical yet meaningful way that produces hope and the potential for dramatic change.

Dr Jason and his wife Jennifer are a wonderful example of walking out a marriage that honors God and in turn fulfills each other. After all, it is far too easy for someone, anyone, to tell you what is wrong in a marriage, but it is much more powerful to give you the information and the tools needed for experiencing a healthy and fulfilling relationship.

In these pages, Dr Jason gives vital truths and perspectives that will build a bridge towards healing and growing marriages that comes from years as a licensed counselor. As you read, you will also feel his pastor's heart come through loud and clear; believing for what your marriage can be.

If it's time for a new beginning in your marriage and you are ready and willing to take the steps needed to move from where you are now, to a place of thriving as a couple, I have good news for you...help is right around the corner.

Pastor Mark Lehmann
Cornerstone Church
Bowie, Maryland

One

Chariots of Fire

"It's how you look at it."
Have you heard your spouse say that, sometimes in utter frustration? If you have, let me give it a more formal name—perspective. And your perspective changes your perception of what is really going on. And until you realize perception is reality for your spouse, you'll keep bumping up against her perception of reality versus your perception of what you think is really going on. This is true whether you are single or married; young or old; rich or poor; a king, a prophet, a servant, or a soldier.

Let me illustrate from a story you may have heard in Sunday school. Be alert to how perceptions change as reality impinges on the discussion.

The king of Aram (Syria) is convinced that he has been betrayed by one of his closest military advisors. After all, how else could he explain that the king of Israel is always one step ahead of him? The king of Aram is furious that someone he had trusted with so much would share with his sworn enemy the private conversations he had in strict confidence. This is treason against the kingdom and punishable by death. Somebody is going to pay for this treachery.

One of the Armenian king's officers speaks up and names the prophet Elisha as the one who was responsible for thwarting all of their military efforts against Israel. In defending his own honor and hoping to save himself from inquisition, he tells the king that Elisha hears from God and speaks the very words he speaks in his own bedroom to the king of Israel. The king responds by dispatching horses, chariots, and a strong force to surround the city of Dothan where they believe Elisha is.

One moment the king of Aram believes he has been betrayed by one of his officers, and then the next he believes he can trust his military might and men and have the prophet of God surrounded. So what changed? The king received new information that changed his perspective and challenged his perception (that he has been betrayed). The *real* reality is the same before and after this new information, but now the king's officers' lives are safe and Elisha's life is in danger...or so they believe from their perspective.

Meanwhile in Dothan, Gehazi is waking up early the next morning to discover that they had been surrounded by an army of horses and chariots during the night. Gehazi has worked as the servant of the prophet Elisha since Elijah had recently passed the mantle to the young prophet and has already been a witness to some amazing miracles. It is some of these recent prophetic miracles that now have put his life in danger as the king of Aram has dispatched such an overwhelming show of force to capture a single Jewish man, Elisha.

> At that moment, it does not matter what the truth is; his perception is that they are in danger, and his perception creates the reality that he lives in and responds from.

Gehazi's perspective is limited as he does not yet see the complete picture, and he fears for their lives because his perception is that they are in danger. At that moment, it does not matter what the truth is; his perception is that they are in danger, and his perception creates the reality that he lives in and responds from. The prophet Elisha is standing right beside his servant and with his natural eyes sees precisely what Gehazi is seeing, but the striking contrast in their perceptions of the situation puts one at peace while the other is in a panic.

Elisha is more than at peace… He is concerned that his servant has not yet learned to trust in the omnipotence of the God he serves. What Gehazi sees as their undoing, Elisha sees as an opportunity to bring glory to God and to demonstrate His faithfulness to his servant. How could Elisha see the situation so differently? Why is he not the slightest bit concerned that they had been surrounded by the Armenian army while they slept?

Real Reality

Elisha's perception is different because he sees something different that allows him to believe something different. Wanting to share his faith and peace with his servant and to challenge his servant's incomplete perspective and unhealthy perception, Elisha prays, "Open his eyes, Lord, so that he may see." Then the Lord opens the servant's eyes, and he looks and sees

> Reality, *real* reality, hasn't changed, simply his subjective perception of reality.

the hills full of horses and chariots of fire all around them, between them and the enemy forces. (2 Kings 6:17) In that moment, Gehazi sees something different, something that had been there all along, and in turn believes something different. Reality, *real* reality, hasn't changed, simply his subjective perception of reality.

Our story doesn't even end there. This massive military army has surrounded their target. The sheer number of horses and chariots and soldiers makes an escape by Elisha a near statistical impossibility, but the math adds up quite differently when you know something that your enemy does not know. After praying to God to strike the army with blindness, Elisha simply tells his would-be attackers that they are in the wrong place, and they believe him.

Despite their training, experience, familiarity with the area, and the fact that they had already seen that they were on the right road at the right city, they cannot clearly see what is clearly right in front of them. Elisha then leads them west from Dothan to Samaria, the capital city of the Northern Kingdom of Israel, where the king of Israel and the king's army is standing guard. The Armenian army is still able to walk, still able to ride horses, and still able to drive a chariot across the mountainous terrain of Israel, which suggests that their blindness is not the inability to see with their eyes (perspective), but an inability to understand what they see (perception). In the words of the Lord through the prophet Isaiah, "...Be ever hearing, but never understanding; be ever seeing, but never perceiving." (Isaiah 6:9)

> ...their blindness is not the inability to see with their eyes (perspective), but an inability to understand what they see (perception).

So, why in the world is a book on how to have a healthier marriage beginning with an Old Testament story about a king, a prophet, a servant and a bunch of soldiers who are all looking at the same situation yet seeing it so differently? For starters, people tend to get defensive and protective when someone comes at them with the truth too directly (as I am about to do throughout this book). Jesus knew that better than anyone and took advantage of the power of the parable to speak truths that could be understood before applying it to his listeners' own lives.

Consider 2 Kings 6:8-22 a real-life parable of sorts that reveals the importance of knowing the difference between seeing and believing something and believing something and actually being correct. Making mistakes and misinterpreting the data presented before us is as old as mankind itself (did Eve really think the serpent was providing helpful information and did Adam and Eve really believe that they could hide from God behind a bush?), and so are the consequences of those mistakes.

This book is intended to be a resource, a tool, a guide to help those of you who want more than to merely survive marriage but would love to experience a thriving marriage. All too many married couples strive to find their "happily ever after" and instead are left struggling just to survive marriage because they are unaware of how their incomplete and inaccurate perspectives form faulty perceptions that they hold to more tightly than truth and reality. The purpose of this book is to open couples' eyes to this destructive cycle, equip them with strategies to establish

> All too many married couples strive to find their "happily ever after" and instead are left struggling just to **survive** marriage because they are **unaware** of how their incomplete and inaccurate perspectives form faulty perceptions that they hold to more tightly than truth and reality.

healthier relationship patterns, and teach them how to leverage accurate perceptions to enjoy a thriving marriage relationship.

The Elephant in the Marriage

In other words, this book is going to finally address the Elephant in the Marriage. We all know it is there, even if we know so very little about it. Where did the elephant come from? How do you repair the damage that the elephant has caused? Why is the elephant such a pervasive part of the marriage? Who's to blame that the elephant keeps growing? What do you feed the elephant and how do you get it to go away?

First you have to name the elephant. I am not talking about calling the elephant Ellie like our children have nicknamed the seven foot inflatable elephant that I use sometimes when speaking on this topic; you have to know what the elephant is and what it isn't if you have any hope of discovering how to protect your marriage from being trampled by the large, wild, overbearing elephant that will not go away.

Perhaps the elephant was there in the relationship before you ever walked down the aisle and said, "I do"; it is also possible that you first noticed the elephant while on your honeymoon or shortly thereafter. You may have been the one to discover the elephant or you and your spouse realized the elephant was in the marriage at the very same time following an argument or in the process of trying to make a decision together. The truth of the

> [Y]ou are now no longer alone in the marriage, there is an **elephant** that **follows** you wherever the two of you go…

matter is you are now no longer alone in the marriage, there is an elephant that follows you wherever the two of you go and we need to give it a name so we can begin discussing the elephant with the goal of asking this unexpected and uninvited house guest to leave.

The elephant in the marriage goes by many names—some more accurate than others. Many call the elephant *unmet expectations, disillusionment, or disappointment.* Others focus on how they feel when they notice the elephant is in the marriage and have named it *frustration, infuriating, or unfair.* These are all apt names, but what we are really talking about with the elephant in the marriage is the truth that you and your spouse are living in two different realities.

The two of you physically reside in the same place in space and time, but it is like you and your spouse exist in parallel or alternate universes. At times the elephant grows as the distance between the reality you live in and the reality your spouse lives in expands. Many feel powerless to discuss the elephant in the marriage because they don't know what it is, what to call it, or what to do about it.

Just like Elisha and Gehazi who were both encamped in the same city but saw their situation and surroundings very differently, you and your spouse very likely often feel like you just see things so differently that one of the two of you must be crazy and it is driving you crazy. Anytime you try and talk about these differences it often ends up in a frustrating argument as you are both convinced that your reality is the real reality. You may have decided together or unilaterally to just keep the peace and stop

> The elephant tramples any attempts to gain love and respect leaving you more damaged each time you try to improve your relationship.

addressing the differences in the relationship, and that is when the elephant in the marriage appeared.

You don't talk about the elephant and you don't acknowledge that the elephant is there, but you each feel the very real pain as you and your relationship is routinely trampled by the inescapable and oversized presence of the elephant. Your marriage is not as happy, fulfilling, or as satisfying as you had hoped for.

You have given up on having a thriving marriage and have settled for surviving. The elephant tramples any attempts to gain love and respect leaving you more damaged each time you try to improve your relationship. This may have been how you have handled the elephant in the past, but there is a better way.

This One's for You

Married men and women routinely end up in my counseling office even after attending a marriage conference, reading a self-help book, listening to sermons, and praying because they are stuck with the same damaging perceptions that caused their marital problems in the first place. Using real-life clinical case examples, stories from my fifteen years in ministry as a pastor, and a ground-breaking spirituality, personality, and marital satisfaction quantitative research study, this book offers a biblically grounded roadmap to help married men and women align their perceptions with reality and restore hope for a fulfilling marriage.

This book was written with you in mind, and not your spouse. While they may benefit from reading it someday too, you will both benefit by you lowering your defenses

> This book was written with you in mind, and not your spouse.

and allowing the Holy Spirit to speak to you through the pages before you. The content of this book has been taught in small group settings for married couples as well as shared before churches and conference workshops of all sizes, but I am so excited that it is now available in the form of a book for you to read and wrestle with wherever you may be.

As the author of Ecclesiastes reminds us, there is nothing new under the sun, and that is true for the biblically grounded truths you are about to navigate as you read through this book. My prayer is not to present something new that has never been seen before, but to present helpful, life-giving information and hope in a way that might make it uniquely more accessible and applicable and might help to shape your marriage into what God has desired it to be all along.

I will warn you up front that at the end of the book I invite you to go back and read it for a second time. I explain why, and I hope and pray that it will make sense to you then and that you will make the time to continue your investment into your relationship. I should also mention that there are a lot of names used throughout this book, and most of them are pseudonyms. I even went as far as to change

> I am not promising you it will be easy—if it were easy you would not need chariots of fire…

just enough information about some of the former clients whose cases I discuss, without compromising the heart of their stories, so that prayerfully they would not even recognize themselves.

Philip Yancey, in his book *Reaching for the Invisible God*, confessed, "I guess I've been disappointed enough times that I simply pray for less and less in order to not be disappointed over and over.[1]" If you identify with that statement, I would like to invite you to consider praying one more time, trying one more time, giving God one more chance.

Allow the words and the prayers of Elisha to speak over your life—that you will not be afraid and that God may open your eyes to see whatever the chariots of fire may need to represent in your life. I am not promising you it will be easy—if it were easy you would not need chariots of fire—but I can promise you that the book you are about to begin will change you and your marriage if you allow it.

I love how Jim Collins put it in his book *Good to Great*, "You must never confuse faith that you will prevail in the end—which you can never afford to lose—with the discipline to confront the most brutal facts of your current reality.[2]" Faith, discipline, confront…I know it doesn't sound like a typical fun-filled adventure, but a thriving marriage can be one of the greatest joys you will know on this earth, and that, after all, is what we are fighting for.

PART I

PERSPECTIVE:
WHAT ARE YOU LOOKING AT?

Some things are loved because they are worthy;
some things are worthy because they are loved

-David Pitt-Watson

Two

Let's Get Started

I will never forget the first time I met Paul and Jami. They were new to the church, having relocated back to the area, and had asked if they could make an appointment with me. I routinely met with parents who were struggling with their child's behavior, adults who questioned how a loving God could let them feel so miserable, and couples who argued too much and hoped I could settle once and for all the debate over who was right. As a graduate student in a pastoral counseling program, it seemed only natural that I would add to my preaching duties the role of counseling those in the congregation who were experiencing some challenges in life.

The State of Maryland deemed me fit to provide counsel. Years earlier, the Assemblies of God blessed me with a very nice-looking certificate of ordination that now hung on the wall behind the seats Paul and Jami occupied. I suppose that by some standard I was considered competent in either role, but I was well aware that I had much to learn. Paul and Jami had such a gentle way about them as they cautiously began to tell their story.

Much like two children venturing out on the early winter ice, testing the ground with each step before venturing further, they carefully and systematically began to reveal what had brought them in to my office. Although I was never any good at poker, my poker face must have been convincing because Paul and Jami took a step of faith and trusted me enough to share their heart-wrenching story.

They started by sharing that I was not the first counselor that they had seen. Their previous counselor had a bit of an unorthodox approach of simply not letting a couple leave until their issue was resolved. This meant that Paul and Jami's last counseling session was a marathon session that lasted several hours at an expense of several hundred dollars. Their first session with me was a stark contrast. I promised them the safe boundary of a forty-five to fifty-minute session that I was going to honor. This boundary seemed to comfort Paul, inviting him to engage in sharing Jami's painful story.

Paul and Jami had yet to celebrate their one-year wedding anniversary and had already faced more challenges than most couples face across the life of a marriage. Jami shared that Paul had joined her at an office party not too long ago. For reasons that were never quite clear to me, a fact that may have seemed trivial at the time, Paul left the party early, while Jami stayed behind. Jami responded by having more to drink than she probably ought to have had, and that is all that she remembered from that evening. According to the police report that Jami filed, the next thing she remembered was waking up at a hotel as a cup of cold water was tossed on her face by a man from the office party. She recalled grabbing a taxi cab home, showering, and then heading to work, having no memory of what happened between the times Paul went home and she woke up.

It did not take long for Jami to begin to suspect that she may have been raped, and that is when she went to the police station to file the report, but this is where Paul and Jami's story took a life-altering twist. An investigation was ordered into the events of the evening, the police concluded that the evening was consensual, and it was Jami who ended up going to court as the defendant. Jami was charged with filing a false police report and was ordered to complete community service. She was also ordered to stay away from the coworker she claimed had raped her, which meant she could no longer go to work and inevitably lost her job.

Jami also lost the trust of her husband. Paul did not know what to believe, but seeing that "the other guy" claimed it was consensual and the investigating officer and a judge sided with "the other guy," Paul found it hard not to think that Jami had been unfaithful. Jami never wavered from her story that she did not remember anything that happened and did not have consensual sex. Jami reasoned, "If you have to throw a cup of water on someone's face to wake them up, they can't consent to anything." Paul's doubts

> One of the challenges that Paul faced was the uncertainty of whether he was attempting to **forgive** his wife or to ask for her forgiveness.

and distrust grew, and their newly formed wedding bonds began to break. Jami moved out, leaving the two of them more lost now than ever before in their lives. Paul truly loved Jami, and it did not take long for him to make the long trip to his mother-in-law's house to initiate reconciliation. One of the challenges that Paul faced was the uncertainty of whether he was attempting to forgive his wife or to ask for her forgiveness.

High-Risk Jeopardy

I have yet to come across a more challenging example of "he said, she said," and one in which the stakes were so high. On the one hand, if Paul were to believe everything Jami said, then not only would he need to ask for her forgiveness, but he would have been the one to have put their relationship at risk, jeopardizing their marriage.

The Bible says that love always protects, always trusts, always hopes, always perseveres, and love never fails. If Paul were to accept everything his wife had said, then he would need to repent of not living up to the standard God set in Scripture. He would have been the one to have violated their wedding vows. Paul also would have likely then set his anger against the legal system that failed his wife, a legal system that failed to protect, failed to uncover the truth, and penalized the victim, forever tarnishing her reputation at work, in the press, and as a matter of public record. Paul would have been part of the problem if he were to accept what Jami had been claiming all along.

> Our **perspectives** are far more important than many give them credit for, and their influence on our **perceptions** is often greatly underestimated.

The alternative is even less attractive. Paul could decide to believe that his bride not only willfully cheated on him, but then broke the law to cover it up and is unrepentant on both matters. Paul would now be married to an adulterous woman who lies, deceives, and simply cannot be trusted. Jami's action that one evening and all of the behaviors that followed would paint all of Jami's actions with a different brush, preventing him from possibly ever trusting this woman he had pledged to love for better or worse until death do them part. Paul was left with a life-altering ultimatum of choosing between two evils, both ugly, both painful. But even more insidious was that he would never truly know what the true truth was.

Paul sat before me, having returned from New England with his wife, seeking guidance, answers, and ultimately hope that there was a path the two of them could journey down that might possibly put all of the pieces back together.

I think it was in that moment that I began to see the power of alternative perspectives. Paul, Jami, "the other guy," the investigating officer, the judge... each viewed this real-life event from their own unique perspective. Everyone involved in their unfolding marital crisis had their own perspective. Even as I am writing this chapter and you are reading it, you and I have a specific perspective, or point of view, that provides us with information on what we are seeing. If you were at the office party that evening and you were serving Jami drink after drink, your unique perspective would perhaps be very different than that of another office colleague at the party who saw her leaving the party smiling, or with a terrified look, hand-in-hand with "the other guy." The honest truth is that you and I do not know what happened that evening, and from our limited perspective we can only know so much. Paul is also encumbered with a limiting perspective, one which will have ramifications each and every day of his life.

Necessary, But Not Sufficient

One of the tasks that I have learned is necessary when working with couples, families, or even individuals is to bring some clarity on and try to identify their unique perspective on the matter at hand. This is a necessary step if a couple is going to successfully address the elephant in the marriage. Our perspectives are far more important than many give them credit for, and their influence on our perceptions is often greatly underestimated.

The investigating officer's perspective included the witness statements, the behavior of the accused and accuser, the evidence that he was able to obtain, and the consistencies and inconsistencies of it all. His perspective provided the objective data, which he then internally processed, creating a subjective perception on the matter. The investigating officer then documented his perception, or findings, in the official police report that was then admitted in court as official evidence. Perception, as this case shows, informs our responses, opinions, and beliefs. What we do in life is because of our perceptions of any given matter.

As people are able to identify the strengths and limitations of their perspectives, they can then begin to challenge their perceptions that were informed by a limited perspective. Jami was able to empathize with Paul's perspective and challenge her own perception of his actions as a husband failing to stand by his wife. As she was able to see things from Paul's perspective, a new perception was possible of a husband who is both hurt and lost. Paul demonstrated tremendous personal strength as he was the first to admit that his perceptions may be misinformed from his limited perspective, prompting him to travel over 500 miles to see his wife at his in-laws' house to try to make their marriage work.

> There are things in all of our lives that we have taken for granted as **truth** that contain very little truth.

New perspectives are necessary, but they are not sufficient in bringing health and wholeness to a person or relationship. A new perspective needs to inform, challenge, and influence one's perceptions if health is the goal. This book has the potential to upend your life like few books have done before, in part because this book is going to invite you to question much of what you have held as constants in your life.

There are things in all of our lives that we have taken for granted as truth that contain very little truth. There was a time when our perspectives informed us that the world was flat, and our perception was that anyone who thought otherwise was wrong at best or heretical or worst. Scripture tells us that God is the same yesterday, today, and forever. God is

> There are very few things I can think of that are more **richly rewarding** than a thriving marriage.

unchanging. It is our perspectives that have changed throughout the generations, from the Garden, to Mt. Sinai, to the Promised Land, to the Cross; our perspectives continue to grow, and in turn our perceptions are freed to grow in kind.

Please be prepared to see things differently, think about things differently, and experience things differently as your perceptions are challenged through eye-opening new perspectives. You will be invited to discover what is trampling your marital satisfaction and learn how to enjoy a thriving marriage. During the time that we spend together through the pages of this book, you will be invited to take an intentional look at yourself, with the goal of better seeing your marriage and the value of your marriage.

Pastor, author, and former college president Dick Foth has always had a unique way of challenging my life ever since our paths first crossed when he was a guest speaker while my wife and I were in Bible college; recently, while in DC speaking to a handful of young pastors, he offered the powerful perspective that there are "two things we will deal with in our lives, relationships and money, and only one of those two will make you rich.[1]" So, from a certain perspective, this book can be a tool that God may use to help make you rich, but I promise you it will not be a get-rich-quick book. Thomas Merton suggested, "If you find God with ease, perhaps it is not God that you have found.[2]" There are some things in life that take more effort than others, but they are also far more rewarding. Seeing the elephant in the marriage is easy, you can't miss it. It is going to take courage and hard work to save your marriage from the elephant in order to thrive, and there are very few things I can think of that are more richly rewarding than a thriving marriage.

Hopes And Expectations

I learned a phrase when I was in graduate school from one of my professors, prolific author Dr. Robert J. Wicks: "Have high hopes, but low expectations.[3]" We cannot ever give up on our marriage and expect it to be a fulfilling marriage at the same time; we need to be open to believing that with God all things are possible (see Mark 9:23) and that our marriage can be more fulfilling, satisfying, and life-giving. It is possible that your marriage is just barely holding on in part because that is where you have allowed your marriage to be. You have neglected it, spoken ill of it, and given up on it.

> When our perception is that our marriage is **unfulfilling**, it ends up withering because of our action or inaction, and this leads to it being unfulfilling.

If you have no hope that your marriage can be any better, then you start treating it as a "dead man walking." Several years ago, my wife, Jennifer, and I purchased an outdoor gas grill for our frequent summer cookouts. Jennifer enjoys cooking outdoors, but after a few seasons, our new grill was starting to no longer look new. We stopped using it as much and cleaning it as much; basically we stopped caring for it, and it became just a matter of time before it needed to be replaced. To be honest, our neglecting the grill caused its premature demise. We had created a self-fulfilling prophecy, much like too many spouses do with their marriage. When our perception is that our marriage is unfulfilling, it ends up withering because of our action or inaction, and this leads to it being unfulfilling. May it not be so with your marriage.

I also invite you to hold realistic expectations for your marriage. Some couples sabotage their marriage not by having low expectations, but by setting their expectations too high. Unrealistic expectations place undue stress upon a relationship, a relationship that may already be struggling. The elephant is much larger than you, and you need to proceed with caution or you and your spouse both might get hurt.

Dr. Gary Smalley addresses the toll of stress on relationships in his book *The DNA of Relationships*: "In general, stress results from unmet expectations. Stress is the gap between what we expect ourselves and others to do and what actually happens... The result is hurt feelings, frustration, irritation, hostility, guilt, and unforgiveness.[4]" Dr. Smalley shared that his stress had kept him awake at night. In addition to causing some sleepless nights for you, your stress from unmet expectations may be keeping your marriage from thriving.

Lowering expectations to be realistic, while maintaining high hopes, can help you prepare for the tough days while creating space for God to move in your marriage on the good days. To be honest, you will likely have more tough moments interspersed with good moments than complete good or bad days. On the other hand, you and your spouse may already be enjoying frequent good days, yet you picked up this book because somewhere inside of you there is a sense that your marriage was created to be something more. Your perspectives and perceptions may be all that stand in the way, and they will need to change if your desire is to move your marriage toward a thriving marriage. I have seen it done before, and believe that it is possible for you as well.

As we begin, I offer you the words of C.S. Lewis from the conclusion of the first chapter of his book *Surprised by Joy*: "The reader who finds these... episodes of no interest need read this book no further...[5]" If you are content with the way you see the world — the way you believe the world is — and your relationships are not in need of any improvement, then this book may not be for you. I suspect you know someone you could pass this book along to who may personally benefit more from it.

Alternatively, if you were drawn to or led to this book because of circumstances in your life, I invite you to allow God to use this tool to assist you in understanding your marriage and other relationships in your life in a way that will invite change. Change is rarely easy. Change requires growth, growth requires risk, and risk leaves us susceptible to pain. We seem to be hardwired to avoid pain, which means that we tend to be hardwired to avoid change and addressing the elephant in the marriage. If circumstances in your life have primed you for some change, let us get started.

Three

Fight Club

S o, perhaps I got a little over zealous and ahead of myself with that final sentence of the last chapter. I have been around long enough to recognize that not everyone is ready for change, and I can respect that. Motivational Interviewing offers catchy names for pre-change stages such as precontemplation, contemplation, and preparation[1]. Because each of these three stages brings a person closer to the fourth stage, action (where the necessary steps for change occur), these pre-change steps are no less important. At the precontemplation stage, people are not ready to make any serious changes to their lives. As individuals work through this stage, resistance to change may be the highest, which is why many people spend a long time there. Hopefully (because it is not as simple as eventually), an individual may choose to consider change in the next stage, contemplation. During this stage, individuals are now open to viewing the pros and cons of changing or not changing as they address their ambivalence to their current condition.

I have met with countless individuals and couples who terminate counseling during these two pre-change stages. They have counted the cost, weighed the risks and rewards, and decided they are more comfortable with their current pain than with the unknown pain that may come with inviting change. The real fun begins in the preparation stage as individuals have decided that they need to change and ready themselves for that change. Keep in mind that all of this work, which could take days, weeks, months, or years, is simply to bring us through the pre-change stages. Change does not occur until the fourth stage of action and lived out in the fifth stage of maintenance.

Pre-change steps are especially important when we are seeking change within a marriage. Husbands and wives frequently enter into counseling not being on the same page. One spouse may be ready to quit, while the other is ready to fight for their marriage. Often times, husbands or wives are dragged into counseling at the prompting of their spouse with no intention of changing. Change within one's self is complicated enough, but when we factor in the different possible scenarios for a couple entering marriage counseling, it gets exponentially more complex.

In a marriage relationship, we could have the husband ready or not ready for change, the wife ready or not ready for change, as well as the relationship itself ready or not ready for change. When we then consider that a husband could be at the precontemplation stage, contemplation stage, or preparation stage of pre-change, and the wife could separately be at any of the three, it can make a person dizzy. I have said all of that to say this: I do not take for granted that as you hold this book in your hand, you or the loved ones in your life are even ready for change. I understand that it is one thing to notice the elephant in the marriage, but is something altogether different to address the elephant in the marriage.

> I have seen God move in so many miraculous ways that I find it hard not to have **hope** for each and every individual, couple, or family who God brings into my life.

STAGES OF CHANGE

Precontemplation:	**Not willing or wanting to Change**
Contemplation:	**Thinking about Future Change**
Preparation:	**Preparing for Change**
Action:	**Change occurs**
Maintenance:	**Change is maintained**

I do hold the strong opinion that change is possible. I will admit that up front. I have seen God move in so many miraculous ways that I find it hard not to have hope for each and every individual, couple, or family who God brings into my life. Today that would include you. As we explore perspectives and perceptions, allow me to have hope for you and your marriage even if you feel that things might be hopeless today. By the end of this book, I believe you will come to see why it is so easy for me to have hope for you even though I have never met you or your spouse. Better yet, by the end of the book, I believe you can come to see yourself and your relationship like you have never seen it before. You may even come to see your marriage in a way that gives you hope, too, like Steve and Beth did.

We Fight Everyday

Steve and Beth's story is far more common than that of Paul and Jami. Steve and Beth were not newlyweds, nor had they had any traumatic encounter that threatened to tear them apart. As is often the case, the reason they came in for counseling was much more mundane, but no less challenging. They walked into my office, and after going through some of the obligatory paperwork, they shared that they fight every day.

I wish that I could tell you which spouse blurted it out first, but the other one was so quick to agree that it is hard for my memory to make the distinction. I also find it difficult to make the distinction between their story and the stories of so many other couples who have shared a similar testimony. What follows is the summary of our time together to the best that I can recall, but I have to admit that now, a decade or so later, I have likely blended together details from enough other similar couples that Steve and Beth may not even recognize their own story.

"We fight everyday" was probably the first thing that the two of them had agreed upon in quite a long time. What I came to learn was that Steve and Beth literally meant that they fought each and every day. Most of the time they fought several times a day. Their marriage was one in which the routine schedule of life was navigated like a minefield. Arguments occurred so frequently

> Steve and Beth were accustomed to using a lot of words, but neither of them had learned to **communicate**.

and close together that it became hard to distinguish whether they had started a new argument or if they were continuing an argument that was recently left unresolved. Steve and Beth were extremely unhappy with their marriage, and Beth finally wore Steve down to a point where he was willing to join his wife for marriage counseling.

When I first met Steve and Beth, neither of them were actually interested in fighting less often. As hard as it was for me to believe during our initial session, neither spouse entered counseling anticipating change. A counselor can usually expect that at least the spouse who initiated counseling may be ready for change, but that was not the case with Steve and Beth. Their motive for seeking counseling was not to change and fight less, but to win more arguments and lose less. They accepted that marital discord was inevitable and wanted to be more successful in their marital combat.

I knew that we had an uphill battle ahead of us just to get to a point of agreement that change may be possible, but I held hope for them that they would one day see what I saw and have hope for more than merely surviving marriage.

We began with some communication exercises. George Bernard Shaw's often-quoted words rang true from the first session: "The single biggest problem in communication is the illusion that it has taken place.[2]" Steve and Beth were accustomed to using a lot of words, but neither of them had learned to communicate. After a few weeks of experimenting with healthier communication patterns, they both became really engaged in the counseling process. Week after week, I would begin our time together by asking them how they were doing. One day Steve responded, "Great! We are not fighting every day anymore." My brief moment of satisfaction in this positive report quickly abated as Steve continued, "Thank you so much for all of your help." Steve was saying goodbye. Steve and Beth had decided that since they were no longer fighting each and every day, counseling must have worked and, like a good round of antibiotics, they had completed the necessary dose.

For a Better Worse

When Steve and Beth had first decided to come in for counseling, they were not anticipating they would leave fighting less. The best they thought they could hope for was to not lose so many arguments. I was successful in helping them formulate the new treatment goal of not fighting every day, but once that was achieved, I found myself right back where we started.

This was not a matter of working with a difficult couple who did not want to change; Steve and Beth genuinely did not know that change was an option. Now, as far as they could see, things had never been better. From their perspective things had never been this good, and their perception was that this was as good as it gets! They were more than content to leave my office that day fighting five or six days a week and to believe that this was both progress and what married life was like. Although fighting just about every day may not be uncommon in many marriages, I believed that if Steve and Beth continued the work we were doing, they were capable of experiencing better.

It actually took some convincing that fighting *almost* every day was not the pinnacle of marital bliss. I invited Steve and Beth to renegotiate our clinical goals and to be patient with the counseling process. They continued with counseling as we expanded their understanding and skill set until the day came, which I now see was all too inevitable but in all honesty caught me by surprise again, that Steve and Beth were once again ready to terminate treatment. They had begun to experience the "better marriage" that once seemed impossible: They were now fighting only every other day. This was a statistically significant drop from our first session, mind you, but still not enough of the "for better" and still too much of the "or for worse" they pledged on their wedding day. But once again, from their perspective, things had never been this good, and their perception was that *this* was as good as it gets!

Some of you reading this book might find it hard to believe, but we went through this same discussion round after round. If I remember correctly, the next milestone was to spend four or more days without any significant arguments. Soon after that, we were able to use some of the same communication skills to reduce the average number of days a week spent arguing down to two. Steve and Beth, just like so many other couples who have shared a similar story, were able to accomplish some impressive progress step by step. Each time they completed a treatment goal, I would invite them to press on a little further. We would set the next treatment goal just a little bit higher, but not too high where they might feel the goal was unobtainable.

Perfect for Each Other

My desire in my counseling sessions with Steve and Beth was to gently challenge their false perceptions that were misinformed by their limited perspectives. They genuinely loved and cared for each other. They were also miserable being married to each other. They did not want out of their relationship, but they did want a way for it to feel less miserable. Neither of them had particularly strong role models of what a healthy marriage looked like while they were growing up. All of their previous relationships had unfortunately fit the mold of what they assumed a relationship ought to be like. It was just a matter of time until two individuals like Beth and Steve found each other and agreed to get married. One might say that they were perfect for each other because so many other people would have not put up with being treated so poorly for so long.

> They genuinely loved and cared for each other. They were also **miserable** being married to each other.

Please do not get the impression that they were abusive and intentionally causing or wishing any harm upon the other. This would be the furthest thing from the truth, but the truth remained that they argued so much and thought that there was nothing wrong with it. They thought that there was nothing wrong with it because they lacked a perspective, a point of view, a reference point that would have informed them that there was anything better to be striving for.

Beth and Steve entered counseling hoping to win more arguments with each other in part because winning or losing a fight was something that they could understand. Each of them had a long history of winning or losing and knew that they preferred to win. Fighting less often was not something that either of them had ever known, and therefore they lacked a reference point that would have suggested that fighting less often was an option. One of the biggest problems Steve and Beth had to overcome was not the content of their arguments, but the limiting perspectives and perceptions that kept them trapped in living an unfulfilling relationship.

> If we can shape our **perceptions**, we can literally change **reality** as we know it.

Holding Hope

It was not that they did not want or long for a healthy marriage; they simply did not have a place to stand that allowed them to see that there was anything better to hope for. As the distance between them grew the elephant in their marriage had become so large that it eclipsed any sight of a satisfying marriage. Poor communication skills were at the heart of their dysfunction and underperforming marriage. Better communication skills were the tools used to help invite the dramatic change from surviving marriage to thriving in marriage, but it was a change in perspective that made change possible. Couples like Steve and Beth are the reason that I can so easily and generously have hope even when husbands and wives share that they have no hope. I can hold hope for them because I can see what they cannot see. Better yet, I have seen what they have yet to see. I have a perspective that informs me that there is a brighter horizon to aim for than surviving another argument.

Henry Ford taught us, "Those who believe they can do something and those who believe they can't are both right.[3]" Our perspectives influence our perceptions, and our perceptions form the realities we live in. I know that if we can have a healthier perspective, then we can positively shape our perceptions. If we can shape our perceptions, we can literally change reality as we know it. The key to transforming Steve and Beth's marriage was helping them see from a healthier perspective. A new perspective can change the world as we know it and bring hope for a better tomorrow.

Four

Prepared to See

It all starts with perspective. A few years ago some good friends blessed my family with a gift of one week at their timeshare in Hershey, Pennsylvania. To this day, it remains one of the most generous gifts we have ever received, and it was a tremendous blessing to our family. People notice if you, your wife, and your three children go on vacation when you are the lead pastor of a small church. When we returned the following week, several people inevitably asked us how our vacation was. Answering this simple question proved to be not that simple to answer.

It was true that for seven days we were able to spend each and every day together as a family, with no phone calls and no emails to worry about. Each morning we were able to wake up free from any schedule or agenda for the day ahead. We spent seven days just being together as a family of five.

One of my personal goals while on vacation is to be so relaxed, so unplugged, so disconnected with what I am supposed to be doing or where I am supposed to be that I lose track of what day of the week it is. If not knowing what day of the week it was were the only measurement of how our vacation was, I could have answered it was a great vacation, but that would not tell the whole story.

We were greeted at the hotel by one of the most severe thunderstorms that area of Pennsylvania had ever seen, according to local news coverage of the storm. My wife and I were grateful that we arrived at the hotel safely, as area highways were shutting down in response to the storm. Instead of unpacking our suitcases and going to bed, we watched severe weather advisories… until the power went out. The storm passed quickly enough, and by the morning the weather outside was fine, but it was the temperature inside that was the problem.

On top of our middle child having a flare-up of her asthma, the entire family got sick with strep throat. We spent the first several days just calling in and getting prescriptions filled. The nearest pharmacy connected with our pharmacy back home was several towns away. One by one we were feeling more and more of the symptoms of the common bacterial infection, and one by one the hope of having a fun family vacation was being lost. I can assure you that most of us lost track of what day of the week it was, but that was primarily to due to the side effects of the medications and of not sleeping well.

From one perspective, it was a great vacation. I got to spend seven days with the four people who mean the most to me in this world. The accommodations were lovely, and the price was just right! I can honestly say that I have never had a family vacation where I worried less about returning emails and missed phone calls, but this time it was because I was too sick to care about messages and too focused on our medication regimen. So how do I answer the question, "How was your vacation?" From one perspective, it was great, and from several other perspectives, it was one of the worst vacations ever. While both answers would be correct, they are both extraordinarily incomplete. It all starts with perspective.

> It all starts with perspective.

Your Point of View

Perspective is a measured assessment of something, especially from one person's point of view. Simply put, your perspective is quite literally your point of view. Your perspective is how you see things from where you are standing.

One of the characteristics of God being God is that He is omniscient. God is all-knowing and all-seeing. God has an omniscient point of view, which means that He can see all things from all perspectives at the same time. You and I, on the other hand, have a limited point of view. We can physically observe things from only one point of view at a time. We cannot be looking out the kitchen window at the same time that we are looking in the kitchen window. I cannot afford to have anyone miss this point, so please forgive me as I go a bit overboard examining the kitchen window. If you are a visual learner, you may want to grab some crayons or markers to draw this out. If you are a kinesthetic learner, you may want to just bring this book to the kitchen and be prepared to walk outside as well.

Let us say that you are in the kitchen and that you can look out over the kitchen sink and look out the window. You may see your back yard, you may see your neighbor's house, and you may even see that it has been a while since you have washed your windows. This is all possible because you are looking *out* your kitchen window from the inside. You could put on your shoes and walk around the house and from the outside look *in* your kitchen window (assuming your kitchen is on the first floor or you have an adequate ladder). The window has not changed, but what has changed is your perspective.

I am sure there is at least one other person reading this who thought, "Well, what if you put a mirror outside of the house and looked out your kitchen window. Would you not then be also looking in your window at the same time?" I would have to say, yes and no. Yes, you would be looking out your window at the same time you were looking in, but only from the perspective of what the view of your kitchen window would look like from the inside looking out at a mirror. The mirror that so magically appeared outside of your window just as I was beginning this illustration now blocks much of your view, and your perspective from inside looking out is now that much more limited.

Perspectives are objective. Perspectives rely less on interpretation and focus on observation. I can say, from a certain perspective, that my family vacation to Hershey was stressful, or, from another perspective, that it was a generous gift. I can also describe a view of the outside world as seen through one kitchen window. If I have two kitchen windows, I can see more and would have a broader perspective, but it would still be a limited perspective.

> **Perspectives are objective**. Perspectives rely less on interpretation and focus on **observation**.

On that first Sunday back from vacation, I was able to see and describe the previous week from multiple perspectives, but each of them was limited. You could ask either one of our daughters how the week was, and you would get perspectives that were different than my own. My wife would have her own unique perspective on the week. It just so happens that we have a very similar perspective on the week, much like we would have if the two of us were standing side by side looking out the same kitchen window.

What the Back Seat Driver Sees

Perspectives are more cognitive than emotional. We observe and assign labels to what we see. Our perspectives inform our perceptions—which we will discuss at greater length in an upcoming chapter—and it is our perceptions that focus on emotionally connecting the dots of what we saw and subjectively formulating what it means to us. At the risk of sounding repetitive, I feel the need to stress again, it all starts with perspective. God's omniscient perspective allows Him to see and know things that you and I will never be aware of.

The driver sitting behind the wheel of the car has a unique perspective that allows him to see out the front windshield, like all of the other passengers, but also has a rearview and two side view mirrors that provide additional information. The passenger sitting in the back seat sees less than the driver and therefore may not understand why the driver has suddenly changed lanes, sped up, or abruptly stopped the car. Each of their unique perspectives provides them with information, from their line-of-sight point of view, out of which they make decisions and form perceptions. Remember this the next time you are tempted to play the role of the back seat driver; although what you are seeing may be accurate, it is more limited than that of the driver behind the wheel.

> Each of their unique perspectives provides them with information, from their line-of-sight point of view, out of which they make decisions and form perceptions.

A Rope, Spear, or Snake

An old Indian parable provides one of the best illustrations I have come across of how a person can be accurate from a limited perspective and clearly wrong when viewed from a broader perspective[1]. I have heard it retold several different ways and applied in even more ways, but the basic premise is that a bunch of men are asked to describe what an elephant is like. Sometimes in the story the men are blind, other times this parable says they cannot see because it is night time, but the idea here is that they have never encountered an elephant before and cannot see the elephant with their eyes.

One by one, the men approach the elephant and describe what an elephant is like. The first man approaches the tail of the elephant and, holding the tail in his hand, he declares, "An elephant is like a strong rope." A second man is near a leg of the elephant and, wrapping his arms around the massive hind leg, says, "No, an elephant is like a mighty pillar." A third man, unable to see like the rest of the men, leans up against the side of the elephant and offers, "An elephant is like a strong wall made from coarse stone." Another man is near the front of the elephant, holding one of the two tusks, and argues, "No, you are all sadly mistaken. An elephant is like a spear, long and sharp." The fifth man is standing beside the very same elephant, yet he is touching the elephant's ear and says, "An elephant is like an enormous dried leaf that has fallen from a tree." The final description is offered as the sixth man, puzzled by the conflicting descriptions as he holds the elephant's trunk, says, "The elephant is most assuredly like a great snake."

At this point in the story, I have read that either the sun comes up or a man who is not blind arrives, but in any event there is now the revelation that they are all describing the same elephant from their own unique and limited perspectives. The seeing, or all-seeing, individual has been used throughout history to represent various things or people, but the moral of the story centers on there being a truth out there that many are unable to see from their limited perspectives. You may have heard that the main difference between humans and God is that God never thinks that He is us. God also never *thinks* He sees everything.

I have been to several zoos in my lifetime. I have a photograph of me as a young boy sitting on top of an elephant, presumably at a carnival or county fair. I know fairly well what an elephant looks like, just as I suspect you know good and well what an elephant looks like, too. So we can all listen to the six men describe an elephant and quickly comprehend that they are all accurate in what they are describing, but inaccurate in describing what an elephant is like.

> No matter how sure we are that we know something, there is often the very real possibility that our knowledge is **limited**.

Each description is woefully incomplete and therefore wrong. They are wrong since they were asked to describe what an elephant is like, not what an elephant's tail, trunk, or tusk is like. Each of the six men possesses a limited perspective, and each of them is able to "know" what an elephant is like only from that limited point of view. I suspect you are already getting ahead of me and have a pretty good idea of where I am going with this.

No matter how sure we are that we know something, there is often the very real possibility that our knowledge is limited. In the parable, none of the six men are aware that their perspective is so limited. Each of the sightless men simply know what they know and trust the facts they have before them as truth. There exists a paradox that we can be both right and wrong at the same time. Many times this struggle plays out in the kitchen as a husband and wife both dig in their heels and argue over something. The husband and the wife can simultaneously be right and wrong at the same time, just like our elephant observers.

Accurate, But Incomplete

You may very well believe that you know what the elephant in your marriage is. You've seen it, bumped into it, have had to tip-toe around it, and you have even been stepped on by it a few times. You may believe that you have it all figured out and you are just waiting for your spouse to concede that you have been right all along, but that hasn't been working and your approach to the elephant needs to change.

Change is why you have picked up this book. Change was discussed at length in the previous chapter, and lo and behold we find that word showing up again here. You may have been thinking your spouse really needs to change when you picked up this book, and I am not going to argue with you on that point because I likely have never met your spouse. I do, however, have *your* attention at the present moment, and there is something that needs to be made clear.

> ...you need to be open to accepting that all that you thought you have known may not be all that you thought it was.

If there is ever going to be any change, it needs to begin with you, and if that change is going to have any chance of occurring, you need to be open to accepting that all that you thought you have known may not be all that you thought it was. Let me say that one more time: Everything you have held on to as dogmatic fact, as reality, may end up not being the complete picture.

You will not be able to remove the elephant from the marriage simply by waiting for your spouse to agree with your limited and incomplete perspective. Steve and Beth were confronted with this truth time and time again. Each time they were willing to let go of what they thought was "as good as it gets," they were able to see that their perspective was limited and that God had so much more in front of them. Ralph Waldo Emerson wrote, "People only see what they are prepared to see,[2]" and some are better prepared by their expanded perspectives. Your perspective on your life, your spouse, and your marriage may be accurate, but it also may be as incomplete as describing an elephant like a strong rope or saying that it was nice for our family to get away to Hershey, Pennsylvania, for the week.

Five

House of Mirrors

W hen I was twelve years old, my parents took me to Disney World for the first time. In fact, it would be the first time that anyone in my family had gone to Disney World. My Mom and Dad had started planning and saving for the trip a year in advance, which gave us plenty of time to prepare for our visit to the Most Magical Place on Earth. Every summer, we would load up the car and travel to an amusement park. I remember going to Six Flags Great Adventure, Six Flags over Georgia, Six Flags America, Kings Dominion, Canada's Wonderland, and countless trips just up the road to Canobie Lake Park, but Disney World was the Mecca or Holy Grail of all amusement parks. My older brother and I decided that we needed to start preparing ourselves for the rides at Disney World by going on the fastest, scariest roller coasters at all of the amusement parks we visited to build up a better tolerance for what the rides must be like at Disney.

Please do not laugh at me. Remember, I said that we had never been to Disney World before. My twelve year old perspective was that if Disney was the largest, greatest, and certainly most expensive amusement park in the known world, then its rides had to be the fastest, with the most inverted loops, and have the tallest and steepest drops and all that made a good roller coaster worth waiting in line for. Urban legend claimed that a particular roller coaster at one of the parks we made several trips to had claimed the life of a teenager because it was too intense for the human body to endure. This, to a pre-adolescent boy, gave the park street credit and made it all that more desirable. My mind could hardly comprehend what good old Walt Disney had in store for us!

Don't get me wrong, my Mom, Dad, and two brothers who made the trek with me to Florida absolutely loved all three Disney Parks, but I have been on escalators that were more of an adrenaline rush than It's a Small World. My perspective on why so many families flocked to Disney World was challenged that fateful summer. All that I thought I knew about the "Most Magical Place on Earth" ended up being wrong. My perspective on Disney World changed, and that changed my perception of the park. We had an absolutely amazing time touring all three parks, but actually being there in Disney World provided me with new information from which a new perspective was shaped.

This is where this book may start to step on some toes. Last chapter, I invited you to be open to the possibility that your perspective may be incomplete, but now I am going a bit further and suggesting that your perspective may not be providing good information at all. What you think you see may not be what you think you are seeing. Our perspectives are the objective, rational observations of objects or events. Our

> If our perspective is not providing us with correct or helpful information, then naturally our perception will be biased and impaired.

perspectives are the literal point of view from where we are standing. Our perceptions, which we will spend some more time with in the next chapter, are the subjective interpretation of those observations. Our perspectives influence our perceptions. If our perspective is not providing us with correct or helpful information, then naturally our perception will be biased and impaired.

Flawed Reflection

Fun house mirrors at a carnival, or on the boardwalk at Disney World, provide a distorted perspective. The mirror image being reflected back to you is not incomplete; it is actually distorted. Most of us realize that fun house mirrors provide a caricature of our outward appearance, and we do not allow those reflections to significantly alter our perception of who we are. What if we did not know that the images being reflected were more than just incomplete, that they were incorrect? What if these distorted reflections provided our only point of view? Substitute a fun house mirror with a mirror marked with flaws. The flaws are not preventing a complete reflection; the flaws are preventing an accurate reflection. This might sound crazy to some reading this book, but I believe it is more common than you may realize.

Let us flash back to Paul and Jami from chapter two. Jami openly admitted that she had several drinks after Paul left the party. We may never know clearly what transpired that fateful evening for the simple reason that one of the two individuals with the most direct vantage point on the evening was chemically incapacitated from having a clear recollection. Maybe Jami had too much to drink, or maybe one of her drinks was laced with a judgment impairing drug; it is unlikely that you and I will ever know. Jami's recollection was a fun house mirror of memories. Her perspective on the events of that evening was painfully marked with flaws and hazy memories.

Steve and Beth's perspective on their marriage was

influenced by the relationships they had seen over their lives. As they saw their parents fight, it began to distort the mirrors that they would one day each use to view their marriage. Perhaps there were siblings, friends, a loud couple in a neighboring apartment, each normalizing the dysfunction and flawed mirror that Steve and Beth accepted as valid. Their primitive instinct to survive conditioned them for fight or flight, and by trusting the fun house mirror for marriage, they chose to fight each other. What they did not see was that God had created them to fight for their marriage and not fight the one they were married to. These distinctions and distortions may seem small, but Steve and Beth came to learn what a big difference a good mirror could make.

> What they did not see was that God had created them to fight for their marriage and not fight the one they were married to.

Most Magical Place on Earth

Even our family vacation was vulnerable to a distorted perspective. As I was evaluating the week in an attempt to answer the question, "how was your vacation?", some of my intel may not have been accurate. As a husband and father of three, I define a successful vacation as one in which the whole family enjoys our time away together. Roller coasters and a giant Ferris wheel were visible from our hotel room, but we never got near either as we spent our time with antibiotics and a giant box of Kleenex. Had I failed my family as a father? Did anyone enjoy the week at all? My perspective was tainted by the illnesses I could see, which often overpowered the smiles and laughter that were still present by the grace of God. Our oldest two children often ask if we can go back to Hershey, Pennsylvania. They apparently had a better time than I could see, from my perspective.

My perspective on Disney World proved to be no more accurate either. I saw commercials for Disney World, I heard people talking about their family trips, and I even saw a few travel brochures. Keep in mind that this was the late eighties and I could not exactly watch YouTube videos of the theme park attractions or take an online virtual tour of Disney World. The information I received was through promotional material or someone sharing memories of their family vacation, and it was second-hand information at best. When I heard that Disney World had the best rides, what I was hearing them say was that Disney had the fastest roller coaster ever, with the most inverted loops and the tallest and steepest drops. My perspective provided a fairly flawed and inaccurate point of view on what Disney World would be like. Fortunately for me, Disney World was still Disney World. It may not have lived up to my dreams and expectations, but somehow the Imagineers who were responsible for the Most Magical Place on Earth seemed to know what I would enjoy even more than I did at twelve years old.

> Unfortunately, too many brides and grooms walk down the aisle with a fun house mirror perspective on what married life will be like.

Unfortunately, too many brides and grooms walk down the aisle with a fun house mirror perspective on what married life will be like. Unrealistic or unhealthy expectations can derail a marriage more quickly than just about anything else I know. Marriage is tough under the most ideal conditions, and no one should ever underestimate all of the work that goes into making a marriage thrive. Ideal conditions for marriage are as rare as that precious stone mounted on the bride's engagement ring. Incomplete and inaccurate perspectives on what married life should be like are far more common — as common as the grains of sand at a beach wedding. If our perspective on what a happy marriage ought to look like is coming from promotional material for a company trying to separate you from your money, or second-hand information from others' memories of what it was like for them to be married, then we are susceptible to erroneous perspectives.

It all starts with perspective. Perspectives inform our perceptions, and our perceptions form the reality that we know and respond to. Incomplete perspectives lead to us forming perceptions that do not see the whole picture, like our elephant in the room. Incomplete perspectives are best addressed by introducing additional information. As each blind man was introduced to another part of the elephant, his perspective became broader and his description of what an elephant was like became more complete. Inaccurate perspectives, on the other hand, are a little more challenging to address. Sometimes we have held onto our false perspectives for so long that we are not willing to accept a new perspective. Accepting a new perspective requires us to first admit that what we once held as truth is no longer true, and perhaps never was. We have discussed how people tend to naturally resist change, and that is just as true when people are confronted with the possibility that their perspectives are shown to be not as accurate as they thought they were.

City of Refuge

In 2010, a close friend and colleague from graduate school, Brian Griswold, and I founded *City of Refuge Counseling Network* as a ministry to provide professional counseling to individuals and families serving in ministry[1]. Brian and I are both licensed clinical professional counselors who were first, and continue to be, ordained ministers. Having both served for many years as pastors, we are all too familiar with the pressures and stresses of being in ministry. Pastors face a unique challenge when they are experiencing difficulties in their personal lives because they often feel as if they have nowhere to turn. Pastors, whether a lead pastor or staff pastor, live their lives in the public eye, a public eye that often assumes that they do not battle depression, do not face marital issues, and — because of their close connections to God — are immune to or above the issues that the people they serve face in everyday life.

That perspective on their lives is as distorted as the fun house mirrors we have already discussed. Focus on the Family reported that 94% of pastors feel pressure to have an ideal family, most of them feel that they have insufficient time for their spouse (81%) and that the pastoral ministry negatively affects their family (80%), and over two-thirds do not have someone they consider a close friend[2].

> The view from the church pews distorts the reality that pastors, missionaries, and evangelists face the same struggles everyone else faces.

The view from the church pews distorts the reality that pastors, missionaries, and evangelists face the same struggles everyone else faces. Pastors are often viewed as experts on God's Word and men and women of prayer, and since they are the people most people seek counsel from first when their marriage is in trouble, they are seen as having model marriages themselves.

Although this distorted perspective on the lives of

pastors may not negatively impact the lives of the people they serve in ministry, it does place undue stress and pressure on the pastors' lives. *City of Refuge* was founded to provide a safe and confidential place for those serving in ministry to find professional counseling. Brian and I believe that if we can help pastors enjoy healthier, thriving marriages, then their entire church benefits, but if they too fall victim to the fun house mirror perspective that living in a fishbowl can create, then they potentially run the risk of being stuck just trying to survive marriage and ministry (or worse).

Sometimes, gaining healthy perspectives takes not only seeing the big picture of a more complete perspective, but also correcting skewed and inaccurate perspectives that have been taken as truth. Sometimes the truth is freeing, and other times the truth can hurt, but no matter who you are or where you live, the truth is the truth, and your understanding of the truth is colored by how you look at it.

> Sometimes, gaining healthy perspectives takes not only seeing the big picture of a more complete perspective, but also correcting skewed and inaccurate perspectives that have been taken as truth.

A Certain Point of View

"A long time ago, in a galaxy far, far away," there lived a boy who never knew his father. A series of events led Luke Skywalker to meet an old friend of his father, and Luke asked him, "How did my father die?" Obi-Wan Kenobi replied, "A young Jedi named Darth Vader, who was a pupil of mine until he turned to evil, helped the Empire hunt down and destroy the Jedi Knights. He betrayed and murdered your father." Luke was armed with information, and let us simply say that he was caught off guard when he learned the truth. Years later, Luke confronted Obi-Wan about this misinformation: "Why didn't you tell me? You told me Vader betrayed and murdered my father." Obi-Wan did not miss a beat and calmly responded, "Your father was seduced by the dark side of the force …he ceased to be Anakin Skywalker and became Darth Vader. When that

> Our point of view can have the power to shape our realities, because it is through our perspectives that we shape our perceptions, and it is our perceptions that create the reality we live in and respond to.

happened, the good man, who was your father, was destroyed." Obi-Wan, sensing Luke's frustration with the apparent deception, then offered, "So what I told you was true, from a certain point of view." If you have seen the movie, you can probably recall Luke's reaction as he responded, "A certain point of view?" Obi-Wan was not fazed and simply said, "Luke, you are going to find that many of the truths we cling to depend greatly on our own point of view.[3]"

Our point of view can help us or hold us back. There is a quote attributed to Albert Einstein that states, "Everybody is a genius. But if you judge a fish by its ability to climb a tree, it will live its whole life believing that it is stupid.[4]" Our point of view can have the power to shape our realities, because it is through our perspectives that we shape our perceptions, and it is our perceptions that create the reality we live in and respond to.

You may be a fish, but do you see yourself as a great swimmer or an incompetent tree climber? The answer we cling to when we ask "How did my father die?" and "How did our marriage get like this?" depends greatly on our own point of view. Abraham Lincoln, a lawyer before being elected as President, famously quipped, "He reminds me of the man who murdered both his parents, and then when sentence was about to be pronounced pleaded for mercy on the grounds that he was an orphan.[5]" You cannot argue with the fact that the defendant was an orphan, from a certain point of view. It all starts with perspective.

PART II

PERCEPTION:
WHAT DO YOU SEE?

"Most birds were created to fly. Being grounded for them is a limitation *within* their ability to fly, not the other way around." She paused to let Mack think about her statement. "You, on the other hand, were created to be loved. So for you to live as if you were unloved is a limitation, not the other way around"

-William P. Young (*The Shack*)

Six

Do You See What I See?

It may all start with perspective, but perspective is truly only half of the equation. Perspectives influence our perceptions, and perception is reality. Stephen Covey wrote in *The Seven Habits of Highly Effective* people, "To change ourselves effectively, we first had to change our perceptions.[1]" The same is true within our relationships, and we begin to change our perceptions by changing our perspective. If we desire to change the way we see things, we may need to first change how we look at them. If our perspective is limited—as with the blind men and the elephant—then our perceptions will form a reality that is based on incomplete information. It is easy to see how this could become problematic. And if our perspective is wrong or faulty, then our perceptions will form a reality that has little hope of serving us or our marriage well.

Imagine waking up in the middle of the night, the house is dark, and you *think* you have woken up in your bedroom. The truth is you fell asleep on the couch. You blindly walk across the room to use the bathroom, still thinking you are in a completely different room on another floor of the house. You are bound to trip over the coffee table, step on your kid's toys, or walk into a wall that you thought was a doorway. Your perspective gave you bad information, and you processed that bad information right into a stubbed toe or a bruised shin. There is a reason it is said that perception is reality. True or not, we live and make decisions based upon our perception of the world around us.

Perspectives are the objective observation of the world around us. Perspectives are the very literal point of view, what we see when we open our eyes. Perceptions, on the other hand, are more art than science. Perceptions are the subjective interpretation of what we have seen. Perceptions are more *what we think we have seen* than what may have actually been seen. Perception is the active process of making sense of sensory input. Perception is far more feeling than thinking. Perception and perspective work hand in hand to provide us with either accurate information or misinformation, but in the end, perception is reality. Your third grade teacher may or may not have liked you, but your perception of whether or not she liked you determined how you responded to her in class and talked about her at recess. Your perception became your reality and influenced how you felt about that school year.

> Your real response to a perceived slight changes things because there can be real consequences to our actions.

Fast forward a few years to your marriage and the same formula rings true. Your perspectives influence your perceptions, and you are living in that world of subjective interpretation and responding to your spouse as if what you think you are seeing is the gospel truth. If you see your wife give you a disrespectful look, you are going to respond however your personality and experiences have predisposed you to respond to being disrespected. You might blow up out of anger, or you might retreat in despair. Your response will be real, even if your perception was based upon an interpretation of an act that may or may not have really happened. Seeing is believing, but it can also be deceiving. Your real response to a perceived slight changes things because there can be real consequences to our actions.

I Hit Something

Carl learned the hard way that his perceptions and subsequent actions had real consequences. People who knew Carl described him as a genuinely nice guy, and from the time I met him until he was finally off probation, he proved to be a likeable man. Carl was respectful, polite, and willing to give the shirt off his back and go above and beyond to help a friend out. Three of his greatest loves in life were the Lord, his wife, and his mother, not that I am suggesting it was in that order. Carl was gifted with his hands and technically skilled working on both boats and cars, but it was his run in with the latter that set in motion a series of events that caused our paths to cross.

Carl was driving down West Street in Annapolis on his way to work one morning, as he had countless mornings before. West Street might not be as well known or infamous as some of the streets in your home town or some of the streets in major cities around the world, but if you have driven West Street as much as Carl or I have, you know what it feels like to try to navigate it and keep your sanity. One fateful morning, Carl was on his way to work when he was involved in a minor car accident. Calling it a car accident is probably a bit of an exaggeration, but two cars did come in contact with each other.

Carl was driving in his lane, and a lady whose name I never did learn was driving in the parallel lane. The driver of the other vehicle was in the process of switching lanes when the two cars rubbed. There was no loud crash or screeching tires to alert Carl of the collision, but it was enough that he knew that his truck had been hit.

Carl did what anyone would have done. He got out of

his car and began to yell and scream and went over to the windshield of the other car and slammed his fist down on the glass one time. Carl did not expect his outburst of anger to undo the collision, but he chose to respond as people respond when they get upset. He hit something. This was not the first time Carl had punched something when he got overwhelmed with anger, but it had almost always been a wall, and it had never been a person. The driver of the other vehicle was not too concerned with what Carl may or may not have had a track record of hitting before; she pressed charges, and Carl was arrested later that day and charged with four counts of assault.

Carl turned a minor traffic accident into criminal charges that would turn his life upside down for the next year, all because he did what anyone else would have done in that situation, or at least that was his perception of his response and actions.

"When I get mad, I hit something," Carl revealed early in our counseling relationship. Carl calmly continued, "It is usually a wall. I never hurt anyone, except sometimes myself." There had been a number of occasions where he had injured his hand when the wall proved to be stronger than the bones in his hands. I can vividly remember how matter-of-fact and calm Carl was as he shared examples throughout his entire life of times when he would punch a wall when he needed to release the pressure and anger that had built up. Carl was now in his early forties as he sat in my office, a really likable guy who was quite reserved and even tempered.

> Carl thought his behavior was normal. His perception was that *this* is how people reacted.

Carl did not look like the type of guy who would fly off the handle and punch you in the face if you said the wrong thing, nor was he that type of guy. Carl was the type of guy who had learned early in life to stuff negative emotions inside and, when the pain from those emotions became too much, find a wall and release the emotional tension with a single strong punch. Cement walls would not need to be repaired, but they hurt far more than sheetrock. For Carl there was a bit of a tradeoff between physical pain and having to repair damage after the fact. What struck me the most was how straight forward and nonchalant Carl was as he recounted decades of hitting walls.

> Perspectives inform our perceptions, and our perceptions form the reality that we know and respond to.

Carl thought his behavior was normal. His perception was that *this* is how people reacted. There was an especially tender moment in one of our counseling sessions when Carl genuinely inquired if hitting walls was what everyone else did. "I got the impression that punching a wall is a bad thing, why?" Carl innocently asked with words that I still vividly remember verbatim. The image that comes to mind is the timid sincerity of a junior high boy asking a girl to a dance. Carl appeared rather meek and vulnerable as he asked, "Don't other people punch the walls, too?" Here was a grown man who had a successful career in a highly technical field, and he had gone through his whole life with the perception that punching walls when you got angry was as common as saying "God bless you" when somebody sneezes. You might find this hard to fathom; I know I was caught off guard. Carl was referred to me for anger management counseling, facing several years in prison if convicted on all counts, but he was now asking me a question that most of us had answered very early in life.

Normal Behavior

Perspectives inform our perceptions, and our perceptions form the reality that we know and respond to. Carl's subjective interpretation of the world he saw around him helped him form a perception of life that included the belief that people punched walls when they got angry. Every time Carl punched the wall, it was a choice. Leaving a tip at most sit-down restaurants in America is also a choice, but it is one that is influenced by our perception that this is normal behavior. Imagine how silly you would feel if one day you came to the revelation that nobody considers leaving a tip "normal" behavior.

Perhaps a better correlation would be to imagine that as you are reading this paragraph, you had to stop and do an internet search to find out what is meant by a "tip" because you have never paid more than what the bill required. Perspectives may be the more objective observation of the world around us; perceptions are the emotional connecting of the dots of what we saw and the subjective formulation of what it means to us.

Currently, there are a little over seven billion people on this planet[2]. This means that there are potentially seven billion different perceptions and seven billion different "realities" that we are collectively living in. The earth manages to continue to spin on its axis regardless of our perceptions, but each and every relationship

> [P]erceptions are the emotional connecting of the dots of what we saw and the subjective formulation of what it means to us.

that exists on this globe is impacted by the differences and similarities in these perceived realities. When Carl's fist came in contact with the windshield of the female driver on West Street one morning, his reality also came in contact with her reality.

The world may have continued to spin uninterrupted, but Carl's life came to a screeching halt that day. Carl's job, marriage, finances, and ability to leave the state of Maryland were all impacted that morning, all because Carl's perception had become his reality and his reality did not match the reality of those who enforce or interpret the laws of the land.

Each and every day, you and your spouse are sharing space on this earth. Some days are without incident, and on other occasions you crash into each other. I have introduced two simple terms in this book that are often misunderstood and misused with the hope that the better we understand them, the healthier our marriages may become. Perspective and perception are not the magic keys to a happier and healthier life, but they may prove to be a vital key to unlocking a healthier marriage.

When to Take a Shower

You and your spouse may see things differently. You and your spouse may be seeing the same thing and walk away with very different perceptions of what you have just seen. Our perspectives on people, places, things, events, activities, or any aspect of life have an impact on our perceptions of the world around us. There

> Every day, you and your spouse are seeing things and potentially seeing them differently.

are reasons you choose to eat breakfast at the point you do

in your morning routine. When you eat your breakfast may be mundane or trivial to you, and it certainly is if we are looking only at a bowl of breakfast cereal. Something happens when we choose to look at life from a different perspective. When you choose to eat breakfast as the first part of your routine, it may mean that you are not taking your shower until later. When your spouse wakes up, you may still be in the shower, or possibly there has not been enough time for the hot water tank to replace the hot water you used. Your spouse is now lying in bed, and his or her very first thought of the day might be about how selfish and inconsiderate you are. Perspectives and perceptions are critically important to a healthy marriage.

Every day, you and your spouse are seeing things and potentially seeing them differently. Every day, you are inferring meaning from actions or inactions that may or may not be accurate. Considering all of the things you may feel need to change in your marriage, perspective and perception are two that hold the potential to give you the greatest return on your time and energy invested. Sure, your spouse may be selfish and inconsiderate using all of the hot water and waiting so late to take a shower, but it is equally possible that your spouse did not want to wake you up any earlier than absolutely necessary and held off on taking a shower until the last minute possible. The truth is out there, you just have to be willing to search for it and believe that you can find it. There is also no better time than the present to wholeheartedly pursue the truth. As author and philosopher Leo Tolstoy reminds us, "Remember then: there is only one time that is important—Now! It is the most important time

> There is also no better time than the present to wholeheartedly pursue the truth.

because it is the only time when we have any power.[3]"

An amazing, relationship-changing event may transpire the day you dare to ask, "Do you see what I see?" and you are brave enough to truly listen to the response. It is quite possible that you do not see things the same way. It is possible that other people do not punch the wall when they get angry. In order to have a stronger, healthier marriage, we may need to begin with challenging our perceptions and seeking to see things as they may truly be. Henry David Thoreau once penned the phrase, "It's not what you look at that matters, it's what you see.[4]" When you and your spouse are looking in the same direction but seeing things differently, you will find it extremely difficult to enjoy a thriving marriage.

Seven

Covenant versus Contract

All marriages are not created equally. The traditional institution of marriage predates modern records and has been a part of most societies and cultures around the world throughout history. In the first century BC, Marcus Tullius Cicero said, "The first bond of society is marriage. [1]" In the United States of America, marriage has been seen historically as both a religious and legal union between a husband and wife.[2, 3] In recent decades, the definition and understanding of marriage have been shifting in the eyes of many with an ever-increasing de-emphasis on marriage's religious roots. Many of the world's major religions that are practiced in the United States promote the lasting nature of marriage, and this de-emphasis on the pairing of religion and marriage has in part de-emphasized the lasting nature of marriage.

The traditional institution of marriage appears to be in decline in recent years, with nearly one-half of all first marriages ending in divorce.[4] However, U. S. Census data from 2009 reports that divorce rates have declined over the last decade in part because many young couples are delaying marriage or forgoing it altogether.[5] This trend in delaying or forgoing marriage extends further back than the past decade; in 1960, 68% of all twenty-somethings were married, compared to 28% in 2006. When asked, nearly four in ten survey respondents (39%) said that marriage is becoming obsolete, up from 28% in 1978.[6]

The suggestion has been made that a shift in the conceptualization of the understanding of marriage has even permeated the Church, as the divorce rate is the same or higher for those attending church as those outside of religious circles.[7, 8] Men and women in Christian churches in America are remarrying at or about the same rate as those outside of the Church. The lack of a distinction between those connected with organized religion and those unaffiliated with organized religion might then appear to be a breakdown in the observance of the teachings of Church doctrine, but it may also further represent a de-emphasis of pairing religion with the institution of marriage. Marriage can be viewed by many as a voluntary legal contract that can be broken under extreme circumstances and, in some cases, as a casual nonbinding agreement that either party can dissolve at his or her discretion.

In the United States, over 2.1 million couples made the decision to get married in 2011, and nearly one million of those marriages are projected to end in divorce.[9] Although the past decade has seen a decrease in the divorce rate, between 1960 and 1980 there was an unprecedented rise in the number of divorces granted in the United States.[10, 11, 12] Approximately 14% of the U.S. population 18 years old and older has been divorced—up from 5% in 1960—revealing an increasing population of Americans who have been divorced at least once.[13] Deciding to end a marriage differs fundamentally from the decision to marry or to remain in a marriage, as it can be a

> Both parties had to come together in agreement to enter into the bonds of marriage, but it requires the actions of only one to end the marriage.

unilateral decision. Both parties had to come together in agreement to enter into the bonds of marriage, but it requires the actions of only one to end the marriage.

Low View of Marriage

A.W. Tozer wrote, "The low view of God entertained almost universally among Christians is the cause of a hundred lesser evils everywhere among us.[14]" I believe it would be equally safe to say that a low view of marriage is the cause of a hundred lesser evils everywhere among us. We can choose to view marriage from our perspective, or from the perspective of those around us, or we can choose to view and define marriage from God's perspective. I will

> I began to see something I had not previously seen. Divorce was just not something that Biblical scholars and commentators historically spent much time writing about.

admit that to see marriage from God's perspective may be challenging, with you and I being mortal and living on earth and not in heaven. By the time you or I get to heaven, the definition of marriage will become somewhat irrelevant, seeing that Jesus in Matthew 22:30 seems to be saying that marriage is just for our short time here on Earth. Perhaps the best way that we can seek to understand marriage from God's perspective is through His Word left for us.

During my undergraduate studies at Valley Forge Christian College, I was given an assignment to create an annotated extended bibliography for a church history course. I was free to choose the topic, but it had to contain 500 scholarly resources written from the Reformation through the modern day. It seemed like a daunting task at the time, especially considering that back then you still had to physically drive to and manually comb through resources at many university and divinity school libraries.

I chose the topic of divorce and the church. It seemed like a logical choice, combining both the pastoral and the counseling areas of interests in my studies. As the deadline was approaching to turn in my project, and my streak of straight As on the line, I became worried and approached my professor. I shared with Dr. Gregory Miller that, despite my diligent efforts, I was struggling to come up with even half the required resources needed, and almost all of them were from the past several decades.

> In the present culture, a person's degree of satisfaction in marriage is viewed as the litmus test as to whether he or she should remain married.

After a supportive and enlightening conversation, I began to see something I had not previously seen. Divorce was just not something that Biblical scholars and commentators historically spent much time writing about. I remember commenting that divorce, like murder, was universally understood within the church, and instead authors focused on the debatable topics like the Trinity, the end times, and water baptism.

Subjective Value and Viability

The past few decades introduced, or at least brought front and center to the consciousness of many couples, the concept of marital satisfaction. In the present culture, a person's degree of satisfaction in marriage is viewed as the litmus test as to whether he or she should remain married. More and more individuals are seeking to evaluate the satisfaction their marriage provides them and choose between investing in their marriage relationship or seeking to dissolve the marriage bonds.

The Jewish and Christian sacred texts both include the stories of Job, Noah, Abraham, Jacob, and Potiphar, which depict some of the tension and strife that many husbands and wives experience.[15] These texts may serve as an archetype of how spouses can endure adversity and still choose to remain married due to their commitment to the relationship that was spiritually blessed by God. However, in the present culture, individuals have the option to evaluate the value and viability of their marriage by their subjective level of marital satisfaction at any given point in time; should that level of marital satisfaction drop below a specific threshold, they often choose to seek dissolution of the marriage. Thus, an individual's marital satisfaction may be critical to the strength and endurance of the marriage.

The Pew Research Center found that for 58% of married couples with children, family life has turned out about as they expected, compared to 21% of those divorced or separated with children. The Pew Research Center also found that 84% of married individuals reported that they were very happy with family

> When we take our eyes off of the Creator of marriage and **His definition** for marital success, we introduce a slippery slope where a hundred lesser evils are possible, if not even inevitable.

life, while half of divorced or separated individuals reported they were very happy with family life. A discrepancy exists between the expectations for marriage and family life and with what marriage and family life turns out to be for many individuals. At the same time, people are finding happiness with family life both within and outside of the traditional institution of marriage.

What did I mean by a low view of marriage being the cause of a hundred lesser evils everywhere among us? When we take our eyes off of the Creator of marriage and His definition for marital success, we introduce a slippery slope where a hundred lesser evils are possible, if not even inevitable. If, on the other hand, we hold to a high view of marriage, we find ourselves having entirely different conversations and dealing with fundamentally different issues in marriage.

What I am attempting to tactfully yet bluntly address is that we may have brought upon ourselves the very marital issues that possibly led you to pick up this book. I also realize that my addressing them may lead you to want to put it right back down. You have come this far; may I encourage you to challenge a perception you may hold that was misinformed from an incomplete or inaccurate perspective that you were exposed to before this book was even written?

Hypostatic Union

The marriage union has been seen as both a spiritual covenant before God and, at the same time, a legal contract between two individuals and the state. In Western and individualistic societies, some view marriage as a contract that is valid as long as both parties live up to their responsibilities. Author and professor of sociology David Bromley suggested that couples who hold to a covenantal view of marriage believe that the marital dyad is the primary unit of the community and that individual sacrifice for the collective good is expected.[16] For many Christians, there is also a spiritual component to the covenantal understanding of marriage that may not be seen in all collectivistic ethnic cultures. In the Abrahamic Covenant it is taught that God voluntarily entered into a binding agreement with a man, which then subjected Him to abide by certain restrictions and uphold obligations for the benefit of the covenant.[17] In doing so, the relationship changed from God-the-Creator and man-the-created to a relationship where God was obligated to bless those who bless Abram and curse those who curse Abram and to make him a father of many nations.

The Old Testament also records similar actions made by God as He entered into separate covenants with Noah, Jacob, Moses, and David.[18] In each of these examples, the rights and independence of God were willingly subjected to the authority of the covenant. From this spiritual covenantal perspective, marriage follows the same formula as two individuals willingly subject their rights to the greater good of upholding the marriage covenant.

God, who is greater than any man or woman, willingly subjected himself to be bound by the covenantal agreement, and this serves as an example for husbands and wives who are created equal. The Apostle Paul even draws this same connection when he writes in the New Testament about believers imitating Christ's humility: "Who, being in very nature God, did not consider equality with God something to be grasped, but made himself nothing, taking the very nature of a servant" (Philippians 2:6-7a). The history and nature of marriage

> God, who is greater than any man or woman, willingly subjected himself to be bound by the covenantal agreement, and this serves as an example for husbands and wives who are created equal.

shares so much in common with this hypostatic union of Jesus Christ—described by the Council of Chalcedon as both fully God and fully man at the same time.[19] Just as Christ was both God and man, so is a marriage both fully before God and before man.

Different Starting Point

Coexisting in a divided U.S. culture are couples who hold to a contractual view of marriage and couples who hold to a covenantal view of marriage. This means that for many couples, satisfaction can be found in the fulfillment of the relational covenant, not just in holding on to individual rights or in seeking to please personal desires, for in their view, the marriage bond is at least as strong if not more binding than its status as a legal contract. There are also some who understand that their marriage works most optimally when the needs and desires of both spouses are equally tended to and that what is healthiest for each of them as individuals best serves the marriage. As Martin Luther said, "Let the wife make her husband glad to come home, and let him make her sorry to see him leave.[20]"

The Christian theological tradition of marriage is rich in teachings built upon the covenantal, and arguably contractual, aspect of the marriage metaphor depicting Christ as the bridegroom and the Church as His bride. Many Christian traditions hold that the first marriage was between Adam and Eve, with God as their sole witness. This idea is still incorporated today in many wedding ceremonies with the quoting of Genesis 2:24: "For this reason a man will leave his father and mother and be united to his wife, and they will become one flesh." The Apostle Paul writes, "Do you not know that our body is a temple of the Holy Spirit, who is in you, whom you have received from God? You are not your own." (1 Corinthians 6:19), and so when the believer accepts salvation, he and God become one. In I John, we read that "[w]hoever does not love does not know God, because God is love" (4:8), and so it is taught that through the loving bond of marriage, we are able to come to know God.

Jesus taught that to be fully human means to be born of love, and possibly even to die out of love. Yet throughout all of the teachings on love, marriage, the relational nature of the triune Godhead, and the Church as the bride of Christ, there is a glaring omission of teachings that would relate to marital satisfaction. This is not to say that marital satisfaction is anti-Biblical, but that marital satisfaction may reside more in the "fully man" than in the "fully God" realm of this relationship.

When we approach marriage as a contract, we expect each party to be satisfied with the arrangement. Should either party decide to, they may at their discretion exercise the opt-out clause of the contract. When you buy a house, you may choose to stop the mortgage payments and the bank will foreclose, or when you buy a car you can choose to stop making your payments and the bank will repossess the car. There are no hurt feelings, because all of this is spelled out in the contract that both parties signed. Marriage is a contractual arrangement between a husband and wife, but if that is all it is, we begin to take on the low view of marriage that I spoke of earlier.

> When we approach marriage as a contract, we expect each party to be satisfied with the arrangement.

Couples who view marriage from a perspective that marriage is a covenant between two people, before God, start from a different point of view that then leads them to different perceptions of married life. All marriages are not created equally. The importance of the role that marriage plays differs depending on who you are and where you live. The Census revealed that 27% of couples in Baltimore are not married, but fewer than 20 miles away in the suburb of Columbia, Maryland, the percentage of couples not married dropped to 9%. African-American women between the ages of 25 and 29 have a 70% rate of having never been married, while only 41% of Caucasian women between the ages of 25 and 29 have never been married.[21] If your zip code and ethnicity impact your perspective and perceptions on marriage, imagine how much your perspective of marriage as a contract or covenant can impact you.

If you have been the one carrying the weight and responsibility for keeping your marriage afloat, my heart goes out to you. If you are willing to try only so much harder and for only so much longer, then your options going forward are limited. If, and I realize that this is a risky and big if, you say that you will love, honor, and cherish until death do you part, then God has a lot more to work with, and the impossible is possible.

A high view of marriage coupled with a high view of God—one that does not limit the power and ability of God—leaves the door open for God to be God and to exercise His omnipotence in your life and marriage. There are much better books written on how to pray and wait for God to answer, and several of them are referenced in the endnotes. This book, on the other hand, will invite you to change your perspectives that may have limited your ability to see how God can work in your marriage and to help you challenge the perceptions that

> A high view of marriage coupled with a high view of God leaves the door open for God to be God and to exercise His omnipotence in your life and marriage.

may have been your reality but do not line up with God's reality. I, for one, vote for trying God's reality.

Eight

Clear the Fence

E arlier in this book, I mentioned that there are currently just over seven billion people on the planet. That number has since increased[1]. About one third of those seven billion are under 18, and between two thirds and three fourths of those over 18 are or have been married. In the United States, a little over half of the adult population has been married. (The number is actually 55% of those over the age of 15[2]; but let's not get too hung up on numbers... We had enough of that in chapter seven!) However you do the math, there are a lot of married people out there, which means that I could not possibly have any idea what your marriage is like, nor could I even begin to understand how you view the world from your unique perspective. Although we may all be coming from different backgrounds, different experiences, different joys, and different disappointments, I believe there can be some commonalities about where we aim to go.

One of my personal favorite quotations from C.S. Lewis is, "Aim at Heaven and you will get Earth 'thrown in': aim at Earth and you will get neither.[3]" I love this quote because there is so much packed into it, as it is true on so many levels from so many different perspectives. This is what I would like us to zero in on at this point: What you are aiming for matters. If we set our goals low, too low, we will never get off the ground. Set your goals ridiculously high, and you just might do some amazing things en route to your goal. With my apologies to C.S. Lewis, I have often paraphrased his quote by saying, "Shoot for the moon; that way you will at least clear the fence."

Some progress is better than no progress. Staying still and stuck where you have been does not help anyone in the relationship. If you are reading this and your marriage has been "stuck" the way it is for too long, may I invite you to consider shooting for the moon? Consider setting your sights high. You may not believe today that your marriage will ever be considered a great marriage, and you may believe that your marriage is as good as it will ever be. I would like to invite you to challenge those perceptions. I would like to invite you to entertain with me, even if for just a moment, that God is able to do something amazing in your marriage. If God could part the Red Sea, provide water from a rock, raise Lazarus from the dead, or feed 5,000 with five loaves and two fish,[4] then imagine what God could do in your marriage if you shoot for the moon.

> [I]magine what God could do in your marriage if you shoot for the moon.

No, I mean it. I would literally like you to imagine what God could do in your marriage. Aim high, shoot for the moon. At this point, do not be concerned with how you will get to the moon, or how expensive space travel is, or what will be served as an in-flight meal. Those details will all come in due time—I believe the answer to that last question is Jell-O—for now let us begin by trying to figure out where we want to go. What will it look like to have a healthy marriage, and how will we know that your marriage is improving?

Every One Counts

In Solution Focused Therapy, clients are often asked what is simply known as "The Miracle Question.[5]" The Miracle Question often sounds something like this, "Suppose tonight, while you slept, a miracle occurred. When you awake tomorrow, what would be some of the things you would notice that would tell you life had suddenly gotten better?" We have not yet tried to make your life better, but we do want to have some understanding of what a better life would look like to you. Sure, you could aim for the fence. Looking out across your backyard from your deck or patio, you could set your sights several yards away and several feet off the ground. Instead, let us aim for the big bright moon in the sky and believe that anything is possible. The distance to the moon is around 238,855 miles from earth, which breaks down to be 1,261,154,400 feet[6]. Surely we can get you an infinitesimal fraction of the way to your goal… How hard could that be? Shoot for the moon; that way you will at least clear the fence.

Years before I was born, Loren Eiseley wrote a series of essays, including "The Star Thrower.[7]" Years after I was born, it began to make its way around the internet, often unattributed and altered, as a story you may have heard that goes something like this:

One day a man was walking along the beach when he noticed a boy picking something up and gently throwing it into the ocean. Approaching the boy, he asked, "What are you doing?" The youth replied, "Throwing starfish back into the ocean. The surf is up, and the tide is going

> Shoot for the moon; that way you will at least clear the fence

out. If I don't throw them back, they'll die." "Son," the man said, "don't you realize there are miles and miles of beach and hundreds of starfish? You can't make a difference!" After listening politely, the boy bent down, picked up another starfish, and threw it back into the surf. Then, smiling at the man, he said, "I made a difference for that one."

There are many miles between you and the moon, metaphorically speaking of course. I hope I have not confused anyone into thinking that I literally want you to send your spouse to the moon, like Ralph Kramden's catchphrase on the 1950's show *The Honeymooners*. I want you and your spouse to stay happily on earth until the Lord welcomes you home. The distance between where you are in your marriage and where you could be if a miracle occurred while you slept tonight may be vast.

There may be many, many miles from where you are to where you desire to be, so many that it may seem overwhelming and crippling. So many husbands and wives never get started down the path of investing in their marriage because they are overwhelmed by the work that is before them. Know this: Every mile counts, and every step you take forward is a step closer to where you would like to be. As the young boy said, "I made a difference for that one."

One Day at a Time

Viewing your marriage as a journey, where each and every step matters, may be a new perspective on your marriage for some of you. You may have even seen a bumper sticker that reads "One day at a time[8]" and applied that to your marriage as you try and survive one day at a time. There is a moving scene in the Pixar movie *Wall-E* where the captain of the Axiom declares, "I don't want to survive; I want to live![9]" What if we were to change our perspective from getting through each day to getting the most out of each and every day, and as a result, we began to build a stronger marriage one day at a time? Decide to slowly inch your marriage from where it is today to where it could be someday.

As we look at our marriage from a different point of view, not only will we be able to see things differently, but we will be better empowered to make different decisions to help us break free from where we have been. This applies whether you have enjoyed your marriage, you are complacent with the state of your marriage, you are discouraged by

> **When you look at your marriage differently, you open the door to seeing things differently.**

how married life has turned out, or you feel you may be ready to throw in the towel. When you look at your marriage differently, you open the door to seeing things differently. Don't forget, it all starts with perspective. What we see informs our perceptions, and perception is reality.

A word of caution would be pertinent at this point. Things may appear to get worse before they get better. You may even want to write that down somewhere you will see if often as you begin to change your perspective and challenge your perceptions. It would be a shame for you to muster up the courage and determination to shoot for the moon, only to get discouraged right from the start and give up before you even truly get started. Some healthy perspective on how change works within relationships would be helpful if we are to avoid unnecessary discouragement.

This May Hurt

As a child, you most likely skinned your knee or elbow a time or two; I know I did. Each time I skinned my knee, I knew what I was in for. When my mom or the school nurse saw what had happened, she turned and reached for the medicine cabinet. I knew what came next, and I knew that the treatment was often more painful than the injury. Hydrogen Peroxide was once the wound disinfectant of choice by moms across the country, and despite the cool fizzing effect on the blood-red skin surface that might normally fascinate a young boy, it was the stinging sensation that I remember most and refer to when I say that things may appear to get worse before they get better.

I can still remember my mom's insistence: "If we don't clean it now, it will get infected." To be perfectly honest, I never really knew what an infected wound looked like. I probably never knew what an infected wound looked like because those around me seemed to always have one of those brown bottles of Hydrogen Peroxide nearby. As my mom would pour the Peroxide over the wound, I would distinctly remember thinking that it had not hurt that much *before* she tried helping. Sure, the knee stung a bit when I first fell, but I quickly got used to the pain and discomfort.

I probably could have even gotten used to living with the pain, since after all, it certainly could not be life threatening. There were times, though, that I felt like I could have died as the wound was being tended to. The sharp stinging pain increased, and then she would use a sterile gauze and wipe the surface of the wound to help remove any soil or foreign contaminants that had decided to stick around. All of this wonderful love, care, and affection was in the name of helping, no matter how much it felt like hurting.

If I have access to a white board during a marriage counseling session, it is at this point that I will draw a quick line graph that starts low and quickly drops lower before gradually building back up to the point where the line started and then continues going up far beyond the initial starting point. The line ends up looking much like a checkmark, and it is used to caution couples that things may appear to get worse before they get better. A major reason that they appear to get worse is because, perhaps for the first time, they are focusing their attention on the injuries in their relationship.

Like me with my skinned knee, many couples have learned to adapt to the pain, and it has become the new normal. The wounds could also be sensitive to the touch, so they have learned not to touch them. Marriage counseling, reading books like this one, examining your perspectives, and challenging your perceptions are akin to touching the wounds. The goal of this process is to disinfect and remove any dirt or foreign contaminants that do not belong. If the damaged relationship is not tended to, it could become infected, and those I have seen too many of.

> Marriage counseling, reading books like this one, examining your perspectives, and challenging your perceptions are akin to touching the wounds.

As Long As They Work

Each and every couple I have been blessed to work with has had their own unique story, but there is an element that many of them share in common. Husband and wife will come in for counseling, yet only one of them is interested in talking. Aleck and Danika were one such couple. Danika scheduled the initial session and came in a week later very eager to talk. Aleck also came in, but that was as far as he was willing to go. As we think back to chapter 3 and the steps of change, Aleck and Danika were definitely at different stages of change.

Week after week, month after month, they came in for counseling, and Aleck sat on the couch quietly, often with his head down and a baseball cap covering his eyes. He remained respectful, and he would answer direct questions with one-syllable answers (okay, to be fair, they were not all one-syllable answers). Danika was encouraged that Aleck was attending, but she was disheartened by his lack of participation. I had seen similar patterns play out before and had as a goal to keep Aleck engaged without putting him any more on the defensive than he needed to be.

Aleck had a challenged upbringing in some rough parts of Washington, D.C. He had learned that, in order to survive, you need to keep your head down and your mouth shut. Aleck had learned through experience that talking about your problems only brought on more problems, and the best way to survive was to ignore your issues and to bury your feelings deep, deep, deep inside. This plan was working well for him until I showed up, and when I say it was working well, I mean that it was extremely dysfunctional, destroying their marriage, affecting their children, and causing him more grief than any man should have to endure.

Life was falling down around Aleck, but since he was ignoring it like a skinned knee with dirt and gravel ground into the wound, he was none the wiser. Here I come along, and I am asking him to tell me how his week was, asking him how things make him feel, and inviting him to talk and to communicate with his wife. I was like a big block of kryptonite weakening Aleck's strong defenses, and he was not enjoying it one bit. The only words of comfort I offered him were that it would appear to get worse before it would get better.

Aleck and Danika's coming in for marriage counseling was not going to be the most fun for a man who had survived by not looking too closely at life. I often tell clients that *our defense mechanisms work as long as they work, and when they stop working, they no longer work.* For Aleck, living emotionally numb and in denial of the world around him as far as it relates to his marriage had stopped working. Danika was fed up, hurt, and broken. She cried out to God for deliverance from this train wreck of a marriage, and anytime she turned to her husband, it appeared as if God were listening just as well as Aleck. That, of course, is one perspective on her marriage; God could see that Aleck's heart was beginning to soften. After several months, I too began to see hope of Aleck entering a precontemplative stage as he showed signs that he might be willing to come out of his protective shell to see the world around him.

> [O]ur defense mechanisms work as long as they work, and when they stop working, they no longer work.

Seeing Clearly What you Want

The final push came after a blow up between Aleck and Danika. I do not recall which of the two did not come home for a few nights after that argument, but I clearly remember Aleck being the only one who came in for our next session. During that session, Aleck finally opened up about how fearful he was of facing how bad things had become in their marriage, how uncertain he was that he could ever live up to the type of man God wanted him to be as a husband, and that's when we arrived at the heart of the matter. Aleck was unsure if he was even capable of loving Danika. Keep in mind that by opening up about these issues, Aleck was not creating problems, nor was he making matters any worse off than they already were. He certainly felt worse about them; he was seeing the problems that he had chosen to ignore for years, and it made this burly police officer cry, but things only appeared to get worse. They were already this bad, but he just had not seen that yet.

Aleck had wanted to "get with Danika" while they were both working at the same large discount retailer. When Danika proved to be a woman of godly character and unlike the other women that Aleck had been with, he pursued her all the way to the wedding altar. Aleck had fallen in love with Danika, but he was haunted by his initial motives that he had never confessed to his wife, and this secret caused more problems than Aleck could have ever foreseen. The moment he decided to open up, to begin talking, to share and communicate with his wife, things began to rapidly change in their marriage.

Yes, things did appear to get worse before they got better, but Danika's years of prayer for her husband had helped her see the man she knew God wanted him to be. Danika faithfully reminded Aleck of who he was inside and the type of marriage they could work toward. Danika set her sights on the moon, and Aleck joined her as they finally were able to clear the fence and fight for their marriage. Each and every step forward they took mattered, and each step brought them closer to their goals. They continued to have their ups and downs, and some significant ones, but the cleaner the wounds became, the healthier their marriage was empowered to become. You and I know that they may never reach the moon this side of eternity, but Aleck and Danika now had a perspective that allowed them to see the moon and to shoot for it.

PART III

TRANSITIONING FROM SURVIVING TO THRIVING

Between stimulus and response, there is a space. In that space is our power to choose our response. In our response lies our growth and our freedom.

-Viktor Frankl (*Man's Search for Meaning*)

Nine

Perspective and Perceptions

There is a cartoon I have seen online where a man is drawn stranded on an island in the first frame. He sees a man on a boat in the distance, throws his arms up, and exclaims, "Boat!" believing that his rescuer has finally arrived. In the second frame, we see a man standing on a boat with his arms also up over his head, looking toward the first man as he celebrates and yells, "Land!" A single-word caption below the cartoon reads, "Perspective...[1]" I was not kidding when I said that it all starts with perspective. What we see from where we are standing has the power to give us hope or to crush our spirits.

Remember, our perspectives are the objective, rational observations of objects or events. Our perspectives are the literal point of view from where we are standing. Being stranded on an island or surviving on a lifeboat after being adrift at sea provides you with a singular perspective. The bad news for our two stranded cartoon characters is that neither one is rescued, even if no longer alone. The good news is that they are fictional characters, and it does not matter what happens to them. You and your spouse, on the other hand, are indeed real, and it matters a great deal what happens to you. Your marriage is worth rescuing.

In order to save your marriage, you may need to be

equipped with some better tools. If you are going to fight for your marriage against all odds, you will need to have some better weapons than what you have had so far. Even if your goal is to invest energy into making your good marriage a great marriage, you will not get there without some change and growth. The saying, "If you keep on doing what you've always done, you'll keep on getting what you've always got" is as true in marriage as it is in other areas of life. The premise of this book is that if you want a stronger, healthier, and thriving marriage, you need to begin with changing your perspective.

I invite you to just try to think of how many times over the life of your relationship you and your spouse have argued or disagreed. Arguments do not have to be big and dramatic to have an impact on your relationship; even the simple and small disagreements can take a toll and have a negative impact on your overall satisfaction with your marriage. What if I were to tell you that many of those disagreements never needed to happen in the first place? Think back to the blind men and the elephant. Which of them was correct?

There is a strong possibility that you and your spouse have gotten into a lovers' quarrel for no good reason at all. You were both limited by your singular perspective and could not see that you were possibly debating for two points of the same side of an argument. From your limited perspective you could not see what the two of you had in common, and focus was thrown to the differences. What could have been a win for your relationship went down in the loss column.

> **There is a strong possibility that you and your spouse have gotten into a lovers' quarrel for no good reason at all.**

Grasping at Elephants in the Dark

Most parents want what is best for their children, and I am going to assume the same is true for those of you reading this book who have children. Having children can certainly increase the potential opportunities for husbands and wives to disagree. Curfew, allowances, bed time on a school night, which video games are appropriate, when to allow them to have social media accounts, how old they need to be before they can date or kiss... This list could go on and on and on and it would still be incomplete. As mom and dad, you are standing beside this very large elephant and you are grasping in the dark to describe what is best for your child.

First-born children have it the toughest because their parents have zero experience raising their own children and they learn as they go with their eldest children. The better husbands and wives are able to maintain a perspective that they are on the same team as moms and dads, the greater the chance that they will be able to reduce the frequency of disagreeing on how to raise their children. You have probably heard the expression, "you can't see the forest for the trees," and it often applies here as well.

The Root of all Arguments

Paychecks typically come weekly, biweekly, or monthly. There are of course those who work on commission who sometimes get paid as they sell, or those who work on tips who may tip out at the end of their shift. No matter the frequency or size of your paycheck, your paycheck means something to you. Your paycheck may also mean something different to your spouse. The money you receive from your paycheck might represent status, security, enjoyment, or control.

The meaning of the money that is yours is another way

> It is not the amount of money that is at the root of these disagreements, but their communication (or lack thereof) over money.

of saying your perspective on money; it is how you view money. If you are working for the weekend, you cash your paycheck, go off to enjoy your two-day respite, and go back to work when the money runs out so that you can do it all over again. What if your perspective on money was that money was for security? You may work all week long and then squirrel away your paycheck, saving it all for a later date. I believe that God must have a sense of humor because these two types of people all too often find each other and then get married.

The number one issue that couples argue over is money. It is not the amount of money that is at the root of these disagreements, but their communication (or lack thereof) over money. There are couples who have more money than they know what to do with and argue incessantly over finances, while there are couples who live well below the

> Your perspective on money informs your perceptions of money, which creates a reality for you to respond to and react out of.

poverty line who rarely argue over money. A dollar is a dollar, but what it means to you and how that differs from what it means to your spouse can devastate relationships. Your perspective on money informs your perceptions of money, which creates a reality for you to respond to and react out of. Your spouse need not be the enemy when it comes to money. But there will need to be some intentional effort to stand beside that large elephant and communicate with each other how you are seeing the same thing, only differently.

Cognitive Kaleidoscope

Everyday life brings with it a nearly infinite number of choices that you and your spouse could disagree on, and you may be predisposed to discount the evidence before you and disagree anyway. Psychologist Drew Westen led a study, conducted at Emory University, which examined the unconscious process of confirmation bias[2]. Confirmation bias is the tendency for people to favor information that they have already held to be true. In Weston's study, fifteen self-described "strong" Republicans and fifteen self-described "strong" Democrats were asked to assess statements by the two parties' presidential candidates while undergoing a functional magnetic resonance imaging (fMRI) brain scan. In each of the statements selected, the candidates clearly contradicted themselves, but the study participants accepted exculpatory statements that explained away the inconsistency of their party's candidate while being critical of the other party's candidate.

Weston's study is fascinating, and I encourage you to read it, but allow me to summarize the study's results by simply saying that the participants heard what they wanted to hear. Does this sound like anyone you may know? The fMRI brain scan results shed some light on just what might be going on inside your spouse's brain while the two of you are arguing

Perspectives inform our perceptions, and our perceptions create our beliefs that, once held, are our reality and may be difficult to challenge even with new evidence.

over parenting, finances, vacations, who left the cap off of the tooth paste, or what was wrong with last Valentine's Day. The study also gives us an idea of what is going inside your brain.

A press release from Emory University quoted Drew Weston saying, "We did not see any increased activation of the parts of the brain normally engaged during reasoning. What we saw instead was a network of emotion circuits lighting up, including circuits hypothesized to be involved in regulating emotion, and circuits known to be involved in resolving conflicts." Weston offered this colorful description, "Essentially, it appears as if partisans twirl the cognitive kaleidoscope until they get the conclusions they want, and then they get massively reinforced for it, with the elimination of negative emotional states and activation of positive ones.[3]"

Perspectives inform our perceptions, and our perceptions create our beliefs that, once held, are our reality and may be difficult to challenge even with new evidence. Weston's study suggests that when confronted with information that is contrary to the way we see the world, our brain activates parts of the brain responsible for emotions and squashes the incoming data and then activates the ventral striatum, which is related to reward and pleasure. In laymen's terms, we may be wired to believe what we believe, and we receive positive reinforcement for holding to our perceptions.

> [W]e may be wired to believe what we believe, and we receive positive reinforcement for holding to our perceptions.

The challenge then becomes to change what we believe if what we believe does not match the truth. Returning to our two stranded individuals in the cartoon at the opening of this chapter, they both held to their beliefs that they were about be rescued. Both men used the data presented around them to reinforce their perceptions, until they were given a new perspective, that is. Once the boat came ashore, the two men were presented a new perspective that then allowed them to each see the unfortunate truth that they were not about to be rescued. New perspectives have the potential power to challenge our perceptions in a way that reasoning alone often fails to do.

More to the Story

Back in the second chapter, I introduced you to the heart-wrenching story of Paul and Jami. Paul and Jami had gone through so much physically, emotionally, legally, spiritually, and relationally that you might wonder what more could possibly happen. Well, in the midst of all that they were going through, Jami discovered that she was pregnant. The timeline of events being as they were left Paul unsure who was the father of the baby. Paul had his doubts and questions before, but now his wife was carrying someone's child, and he did not know whose it was. Many pregnancies bring with them a certain level of concern or anxiety, but for Paul, a lot more was riding on the answer to the question, "Whose eyes would the baby have?"

Just like when our fictional castaway landed upon the shore in our cartoon, our real-life husband was about to have a new perspective thrust upon him when Jami's baby was born. In an instant, our shipwrecked character went from lost at sea, about to be saved sighting land, and right to stranded on a desert island. Paul went from a husband lost, not knowing if he could trust his wife, to a husband unsure if he was about to be the father of his first-born child or if his wife was about to give birth to another man's baby.

To Paul's credit, he trusted God, and God answered his

prayers when Jami gave birth to a baby girl who was absolutely Paul's child. So many doubts, so many concerns, so many questions that Paul had about the baby were answered as he held her in his arms. There was no amount of reasoning or explaining that was more powerful in convincing Paul that Jami was carrying his child than to hold her in his own arms.

Connecting Paul and Jami's child to Westen's study at Emory University, there are those who would have been predisposed to trust or not trust that Jami had been faithful to Paul. Those personally held perceptions would have been reinforced by any amount of perceived evidence over the remaining nine months of her pregnancy, and any observations that were contrary to the existing perceptions would likely have been minimized or disregarded. It would not be until a new perspective was granted, such as being able to see Paul's reflection in the baby's eyes or hearing the results of a paternity test, that the existing perceptions could be challenged.

Most couples are not faced with such a dramatic crisis to resolve, yet so many marriages are facing the potential crisis of not resolving their different perspectives. Disagreeing over the best flavor of ice cream is trivial, but working against each other and failing to work together erodes the strength of a marriage. Even when husbands and wives are unable to see eye to eye, they need to be able to stand side by side so that they are at least able to look at the problem from the same perspective, increasing their chances of holding similar perceptions. Our two cartoon characters may not have been delivered, but at least now neither of them is alone. If they can work together, they will be far better equipped for what life throws at them next.

Ten

"He Said, She Said"

I have spent thousands of hours working with couples navigating the age-old game of "He Said, She Said." And I am here to tell you that it is a fool's errand trying to get to the bottom of who said what. Why? Because our perspectives allowed us to hear only a portion of what was said, and then our perceptions have tainted what made it through. Do you recall Steve and Beth who we met earlier in chapter three? Steve and Beth were the couple who came in for counseling because they fought every day.

What kept Steve and Beth trapped was holding on to the belief that what they saw was all that there was to see, and what they thought they saw and experienced was reality. I am here to share with you some helpful news: Very few of us live in reality. Mark Twain (as quoted by Les Parrott) perhaps said it best when reflecting on childhood: "When I was seven, my father knew everything. When I was fourteen, my father knew nothing. But when I was twenty-one, I was amazed how much the old man had learned in just seven years.[1]"

Our ability to recall details of events and conversations (accurately!) is rarely as good as we may give ourselves credit. I love how Albert Einstein put it: "Memory is deceptive because it is colored by today's events.[2]" Couples spend far too much time and energy arguing over who said what to whom and what was meant by it then and why it was said in the first place, or if it was ever said at all.

You have likely heard the saying, "There are always three sides to a story: his side, her side, and the truth." There is some truth to that, but it is also far more complicated than that. Let us look at the following example, and just in case you might feel I am talking about you: "The events depicted in this vignette are fictitious. Any similarity to any person, living or dead, is merely coincidental."

> ...our perspectives allowed us to hear only a portion of what was said, and then our perceptions have tainted what made it through.

Danger Ahead

Brandon and Amber are a young couple who have been married for a few years. They met early on in college, started dating their freshmen year, and got married shortly after graduation. They do not have any children yet as they are focusing on establishing their careers and their relationship.

They are driving to church on the final Sunday morning in May as Amber begins thinking through the week and asks out loud, "Do we have any plans for Friday night?"

It is twenty-five minutes past the hour, so Brandon is behind the wheel engrossed in listening to the sports update as he is trying to figure out who the starting pitcher would be that afternoon. He does not hear Amber's question, so obviously he does not respond.

Brandon does not respond, so obviously Amber wonders why. Amber knows that Friday is their anniversary and says to herself: *I bet he has forgotten again*. The truth is that he has never had a chance to forget since Amber has planned each anniversary since they started dating.

The radio station does not mention starting pitchers, but three minutes have now passed and the radio has moved on to the weather report. It is going to rain. Brandon is a little annoyed. He also notices that Amber is looking a little annoyed and thinks: *That's odd, why would she care that it is going to rain this afternoon?* He decides to switch the radio back to music, hoping a good praise song might help cheer up Amber.

It does not help. Amber now says to herself: *I cannot believe he just did that. He so knows he is in trouble for forgetting our anniversary and does not want to deal with it. Now he is just turning on music to tune me out.* Amber's eyes begin to water.

Brandon is realizing that it has been several minutes since the last time he and Amber have said anything. He turns to her to say something, notices that she looks like she is about to cry, and thinks to himself: *Wow, I never knew this song was so powerful. I prefer that dude with the accent who sings that song about something, but put on a worship song with a high-pitched female worship leader, and my wife gets all misty eyed.* Brandon quickly looks away out of respect for his wife's personal space and her time with the Lord.

> I prefer that dude with the accent who sings that song about something, but put on a worship song with a high-pitched female worship leader, and my wife gets all misty eyed.

Amber notices how quickly Brandon diverted his eyes when she went to look at him, and her misty eyes become full tears as she thinks to herself: *He can't even look me in the eye! What a coward! He would never forget the starting time of his precious baseball game, but could he be bothered to remember the anniversary of the day he pledged his love to me?*

Brandon is now really confused and says to himself: *I cannot think for the life of me what his name is. He might be Australian, or British, but he sings that song about that thing. I wish I could ask Amber, she always knows these types of things. But I'm just going to keep quiet and let her have this time with God. I bet I'm making one big fat deposit into her love bank this morning! I am being so considerate of her feelings.*

Amber is about to explode and says to God: *Brandon is so inconsiderate; he never cares about my feelings. He knows that I am mad at him, and he does not have the courage to admit that he forgot about our anniversary, again.*

Brandon's train of thought is quickly interrupted as he remembers the bank: *I have to get to the bank! Every year Amber makes these amazing anniversary surprise plans, and I need to make sure we have enough money to cover whatever she has in store for this year. I know she enjoys planning them so much, but I wish that one year she would let me pick what we get to do.* As they pull into the church parking lot, Brandon says to himself: *I guess, in a sense, my gift to Amber is that I give her carte blanche to make the evening memorable and meaningful to her.* That thought made Brandon smile.

Amber notices the smile and is hurt: *He thinks he is off the hook just because we are at church!* She says to him, "I bet you are glad we are at church."

"Yes," Brandon offers, a little confused by the question, or was it a comment? "But sometimes it can feel like church, even right here in the car," he continues.

It is a bit of an awkward comment for Brandon, but he does not quite know what else to say. He has always admired Amber's spiritual sensitivity and does not want her looking down on him for not being as spiritually moved by the song earlier in the car ride.

Amber immediately opens the door and begins to storm across the parking lot, hoping to find a comforting friend to rescue her from this morning's nightmare.

Brandon breathes a sigh of relief that he played the situation off so well and, seeing only Amber's eagerness to walk toward church, is about to get out of the car and follow her. Just as he is about to turn off the car, he hears the introduction to a song that he thinks is by that guy with the accent. He lingers in the car for just a few seconds longer and then realizes that it is only a commercial.

Brandon steps out of the car and says out loud, "I am never going to figure it out. It is like a foreign language to me. Oh well, I guess it is not really that important."

"Not really important?" Ambers replies as she is stopped dead in her tracks halfway across the parking lot.

"No, you know me. You win some and you lose some," Brandon quips. "Hey, do we have any plans for Friday night?"

You Lose Just for Playing

If only we could all have reality television crews follow us around all day, every day. If only we could have every minute of every day available to play back like instant replay. If only we also had a video confessional where we could also air our thoughts and clarify our actions, but that is not real life. What we are left with instead is the classic game of "He Said, She Said," where everybody who chooses

> What we are left with instead is the classic game of "He Said, She Said," where everybody who chooses to play loses.

to play loses.

We lose because we do not know that the rules are stacked against us from ever winning. Okay, to be fair, some people might win, but with Las Vegas-style odds, you will almost end up losing more just by playing. Those who chose to play need to be aware that the risks are great and the odds of coming out ahead are exceedingly slim. If Brandon and Amber were to attempt to play "He Said, She Said," they would not get very far, and it is far more likely that it would only cause more problems.

You and your spouse may never have experienced a car ride like Brandon and Amber's, but I am sure you can imagine what it would be like for them to try to untangle how much went wrong and where it went wrong. Who was at fault? Be careful how you answer that rhetorical question, as it may reveal your bias. Should Brandon have been listening more carefully, or should Amber have known not to try to talk to Brandon during the sports update?

Whose fault is it that Brandon has yet to plan an anniversary celebration? The easy answer might be Brandon, but is Amber partially culpable for her own dissatisfaction by not giving Brandon a chance to plan an anniversary? "Brandon has never planned an anniversary" is true, but no more true than saying "Brandon has planned every anniversary that Amber has allowed him to."

That is assuming that planning the anniversary is even the main issue. Is it finances, the time Brandon spends on sports, Brandon's poor memory (relative to Amber), or a laissez-faire approach to his marriage? Did Brandon experience an over controlling father growing up that he is trying to overcompensate for in his marriage, or did Amber witness two parents who lacked affection in their short-lived marriage? As we can quickly see, who said what is just the tip of the iceberg. The Titanic did not sink because of the tip of the iceberg; the Titanic sank because of the damage done by what was unseen below the surface.

Welcome to Earth

When we play "He Said, She Said," our perspectives allow us to hear only a portion of what was said, and our perceptions taint the memories of what made it through. If you are one of the millions who have read books like *Men are from Mars, Women are from Venus*[3], you may be under the impression that men act one way and women act another way. You may have even identified with Brandon or Amber based on gender and saw yourself in their seat, and that may have made the other seat appear to be the one at fault. It is okay to admit this if it is true for you; no one will ever know. I would like to suggest that if this is true for you, it may not be helping your marriage be the marriage you dream of.

> When we play "He Said, She Said," our perspectives allow us to hear only a portion of what was said, and our perceptions taint the memories of what made it through.

Sure there are differences between men and women, but we are not from different planets. A University of Rochester study—playfully titled *Men are from ~~Mars~~ Earth, women are from ~~Venus~~ Earth*—found that, "[f]rom empathy and sexuality to science inclination and extroversion, statistical analysis of 122 different characteristics involving 13,301 individuals finds that men and women, by and large, do not fall into different groups.[4]" There are differences between you and your spouse, and the differences may be more powerful than mere gender. The main difference between you and your spouse is that the two of you live in different and unique realities. Perspectives inform your perception, and your perceptions create your reality. You and your spouse are from the same planet; you just live in different worlds.

Instead of trying to place blame or untangle a twisted conversation, focus on trying to get to know your spouse better. Charles T. Lee offers some practical words of wisdom in his book *Good Idea. Now What?* "Most of the conflict is fictional and imaginary. It is not rooted in reality. It's more perception than fact. No one knows the whole story.[5]" No one will ever know the whole story just by replaying a blow-by-blow account of something that has happened in the past. Our perspectives are too limited, and our perceptions are too tainted. What is needed is a better way to cut

> You and your spouse are from the same planet; you just live in different worlds.

through the imaginary world that we have accepted as reality and to see things more as they truly are.

Accepting the truth that no one knows the whole story is a necessary, but not sufficient, condition for change. We need to be willing to try something new. You have no doubt already been on this planet for a while... years, decades, even several decades. You have already figured out many things about living on this third rock from the Sun that we get to call our home for this short sliver of eternity. Over the remaining chapters of this book, I am going to ask you to question, challenge, and possibly even change much of what you have come to learn. You may still keep your favorite dessert or preferred way of getting toothpaste out of the tube, and I will not ask you to change your opinion on the best love songs of all time, but how you look at things, what things to look at in the first place, how to communicate, how to listen, how to express and receive love, and even the definition of what is a healthy marriage are all up for grabs. Consider this your final warning; you may never look at life the same way again.

Eleven

Allegory of the Cave

Many reading this book may already be familiar with Plato's *Allegory of the Cave*[1]. Many more may be familiar with the 1999 Academy Award-winning movie *The Matrix*, which was inspired by Plato's *Allegory of the Cave* and depicts many of the allegory's central themes and ideas. The thirty-second synopsis of both the short story and the movie is that the world we live in is but a poor reflection, a copy, of the real world that we have yet to be made aware of.

The Apostle Paul, who never watched *The Matrix*, but no doubt was familiar with Plato's writing, used a similar metaphor when he wrote to the church in Corinth, "For now we see through a glass, darkly; but then face to face: now I know in part; but then shall I know even as also I am known" (1 Corinthians 13:12, KJV). While many Christian believers have become aware of God's unseen hand in their lives and of their future hope of leaving this world behind and seeing God face to face one day, many still live their lives on earth like the prisoners Plato wrote about in his *Allegory of the Cave*.

Book VII

The *Allegory of the Cave* appears in Book VII of Plato's best-known work, *The Republic*, which was written around 380 B.C. Plato's writings are in the form of a dialogue, with Socrates as the central speaker. The *Allegory of the Cave* is a dialogue between Plato's brother Glaucon and his mentor Socrates. I suggest you try envisioning the scene that Plato describes in the following excerpt. If you have any artistic skills, you may want to try sketching out the scene on a blank page in this book, or do a quick search online for one of countless illustrations of the *Allegory of the Cave*. Here is the scene:

> [**Socrates**] "And now, I said, let me show in a figure how far our nature is enlightened or unenlightened: --Behold! human beings living in a underground cave, which has a mouth open towards the light and reaching all along the cave; here they have been from their childhood, and have their legs and necks chained so that they cannot move, and can only see before them, being prevented by the chains from turning round their heads. Above and behind them a fire is blazing at a distance, and between the fire and the prisoners there is a raised way; and you will see, if you look, a low wall built along the way, like the screen which marionette players have in front of them, over which they show the puppets."
>
> [**Glaucon**] "I see."
>
> [**Socrates**] "And do you see, I said, men passing along the wall carrying all sorts of vessels, and statues and figures of animals made of wood and stone and various materials, which appear over the wall? Some of them are talking, others silent."
>
> [**Glaucon**] "You have shown me a strange image, and they are strange prisoners."
>
> [Socrates] "Like ourselves, I replied; and they see only their own shadows, or the shadows of one another, which the fire throws on the opposite wall of the cave?"

The scenario that Socrates is describing to Glaucon is a bit of an odd one. If Plato were writing this same allegory today, he could have simply described people in a movie theater chained so that they could see only the projection screen and who believed that what they saw on the screen was real, unaware of the projector casting images upon the wall. Plato is suggesting to the reader that everything that is seen and known may not be all that there is.

> The shadows are all that they have ever known, and from their limited perspective, their perception of what they see becomes their reality.

The prisoners have a limited perspective where they can see only the shadows that are cast upon the wall of the cave, and since that is all they can see, they come to believe that the shadows are more than the mere shadows of statues and figures that you and I understand them to be. The prisoners perceive that these shadows are real. Socrates goes on to say:

> "And suppose further that the prison heard an echo which came from the other side, would they not be sure to fancy when one of the passers-by spoke that the voice which they heard came from the passing shadow?"

Even the very sounds that the prisoners heard are misattributed to the shadows. Who could blame them? The shadows are all that they have ever known, and from their limited perspective, their perception of what they see becomes their reality. Socrates offers the following chilling statement:

"To them, I said, the truth would be literally nothing but the shadows of the images."

Many husbands and wives go through their lives as prisoners in a cave with their heads stuck looking at the world a certain way. The chains are not literal iron chains, but the chains are stubbornness, ignorance, ambivalence, poor role models, lack of experience, or unhealthy expectations. They are trapped and see the world only from a limited perspective, and then they are left to make sense of all of the sights and sounds they experience. Remember, as Henry David Thoreau put it, "It's not what you look at that matters, it's what you see.[2]"

Making Sense of It

Why did he come home late? He must be cheating on me. Why did she choose a seafood restaurant over a steak house? She is being so selfish! How come he remembers our daughter's birthday but forgot our anniversary? He must love her more than me. Why does she wake up early in the morning to take the dog for a walk? She must be avoiding me...

We have to make sense of what we are looking at. You and I do it each and every day, all day long. Sometimes we are correct, and all too often we are not. As long as we are prisoners in the cave, we are convinced that we are correct. All the evidence we have in front of us supports that we are correct, even when we are sadly mistaken. This is one of the things I have always found chilling about

> As long as we are stuck with our limiting perspective, we can create an entire alternate reality and comfortably call it our home.

Plato's allegory: that we can be certain that we are correct and can even be able to explain, defend, and convince others that we are correct, yet still be so wrong. As long as we are stuck with our limiting perspective, we can create an entire alternate reality and comfortably call it our home. That is, until a new perspective sets us free:

> [**Socrates**] "And now look again, and see what will naturally follow if the prisoners are released and disabused of their error. At first, when any of them is liberated and compelled suddenly to stand up and turn his neck round and walk and look towards the light, he will suffer sharp pains; the glare will distress him, and he will be unable to see the realities of which in his former state he had seen the shadows; and then conceive some one [sic] saying to him, that what he saw before was an illusion, but that now, when he is approaching nearer to being and his eye is turned towards more real existence, he has a clearer vision, -what will be his reply? And you may further imagine that his instructor is pointing to the objects as they pass and requiring him to name them, -will he not be perplexed? Will he not fancy that the shadows which he formerly saw are truer than the objects which are now shown to him?"
>
> [**Glaucon**] "Far truer."
>
> [**Socrates**] "And if he is compelled to look straight at the light, will he not have a pain in his eyes which will make him turn away to take and take in the objects of vision which he can see, and which he will conceive to be in reality clearer than the things which are now being shown to him?"

You may be feeling the same way as you are reading this book today: in pain, distressed, and perplexed. I am inviting you to be liberated from being able to view your marriage and the world around you only from a single limiting perspective. Are you open to being compelled to suddenly stand up and take a metaphorical look around for the first time? I am inviting you to look toward the light that has remained out of your line of sight and see truths that are more real than the shadows that have kept you company since childhood. There is a turning point that Socrates goes on to speak of, when you can no longer go back to accepting the former shadows as realities because you have seen something far truer.

Dragged Towards the Light

Socrates also warns of pain and discomfort. The natural reaction to being exposed to the painful bright light is to turn away and avert your eyes. It will be much easier for you to put this book down, avert your eyes, and hold to the shadows as reality. The shadows are what you have known, and they are much clearer to you. The shadows are much clearer as long as you stay in the cave and are not looking at new truths being shown to you.

> The shadows are much clearer as long as you stay in the cave and are not looking at new truths being shown to you.

[**Socrates**] And suppose once more, that he is reluctantly dragged up a steep and rugged ascent, and held fast until he's forced into the presence of the sun himself, is he not likely to be pained and irritated? When he approaches the light his eyes will be dazzled, and he will not be able to see anything at all of what are now called realities.

[**Glaucon**] Not all in a moment, he said.

[**Socrates**] He will require to grow accustomed to the sight of the upper world. And first he will see the shadows best, next the reflections of men and other objects in the water, and then the objects themselves; then he will gaze upon the light of the moon and the stars and the spangled heaven; and he will see the sky and the stars by night better than the sun or the light of the sun by day?

[**Glaucon**] Certainly.

[**Socrates**] Last of all he will be able to see the sun, and not mere reflections of him in the water, but he will see him in his own proper place, and not in another; and he will contemplate him as he is.

I have worked with more than one spouse who has been reluctantly dragged up a steep and rugged ascent by situations in life. Not everyone makes it to the presence of the sun. If you get too pained or irritated, you may choose to put this book back down, and couples sometimes choose to quit counseling and return to the metaphorical cave.

> There is far too much at stake in your life, your marriage, and your family to turn back now.

Other individuals, however, do press through the discomfort and are able to see the stars, the moon, and the sun for the first time. Socrates says, "…and he will contemplate him as he is."

I choose to believe that God has brought this book into your hands for a purpose and has helped you get this far so that you will be among the success stories. There is far too much at stake in your life, your marriage, and your family to turn back now. I guarantee you, there will be some uncomfortable moments in the chapters ahead, but I can also guarantee you that the rewards will far outweigh the temporal discomfort of adjusting to the true light of day.

You already know that the road ahead may be difficult. There will be numerous opportunities to bury your head in the sand, say "enough is enough," and attempt to go back to the way things were before, but you will never truly be able to. This is because you now know, or at least are beginning to realize, that some of the distress in your marriage has been caused by your limiting perspective and false perceptions.

Better to Be Blinded or Not Able To See?

Take a deep breath, relax, and pace yourself. It has taken you your entire life to get to this point, and it is reasonable to anticipate that any significant and meaningful change will also take some time. In the movie *The Matrix,* Neo takes the red pill, and his eyes are instantly opened to realities he never knew existed. In Plato's *Allegory of the Cave,* the prisoner has a slower ascent to the surface. In your life it may take time, and your eye opening may come incrementally. What matters is that you move from where you are today to where God desires for you to be tomorrow, and in order to get there, you need to outgrow a limiting perspective and some false perceptions.

There is no pill that you can take to open your eyes and immediately resolve the false perceptions in your life or in your marriage, and you seeing things more clearly does not automatically translate into your spouse or your family also having their eyes opened. Socrates continues:

> [**Socrates**] "And if there were a contest, and he had to compete in measuring the shadows with the prisoners who had never moved out of the cave, while his sight was still weak, and before his eyes

had become steady (and the time which would be needed to acquire this new habit of sight might be very considerable) would he not be ridiculous? Men would say of him that up he went and down he came without his eyes; and that it was better not even to think of ascending; and if any one tried to loose another and lead him up to the light, let them only catch the offender, and they would put him to death."

We tend to get extremely attached to the realities we live in, even if those realities are the source of endless misery. People have an amazing affinity toward maintaining homeostasis, and it may be that very tendency that has kept you and your marriage stuck where it is and not becoming all that you long for it to be. In his book, *Mastery,* George Leonard explains how homeostasis will prevent us from making drastic changes and how we will fight to maintain stability even if it is detrimental to us:

> We tend to get extremely attached to the realities we live in, even if those realities are the source of endless misery.

Every one of us resists significant change, no matter whether it's for the worse or for the better. Our body, brain and behavior have a built-in tendency to stay the same within rather narrow limits, and to snap back when changed...Be aware of the way homeostasis works...Expect resistance and backlash. Realize that when the alarm bells start ringing, it doesn't necessarily mean you're sick or crazy or lazy or that you've made a bad decision in embarking on the journey of mastery. In fact, you might take these signals as an indication that your life is definitely changing–just what you've wanted.... Be willing to negotiate with your resistance to change.[3]

So, if you are ready to break free from your chains and escape from the cave, then follow me. If you are willing to negotiate with your resistance, true and meaningful change awaits you. Remember, I am not speaking about changing your spouse, but changing you. Changing the way you see the world, the way you see yourself in the world, and the way you interact with and respond to your spouse.

> If you are willing to negotiate with your resistance, true and meaningful change awaits you.

Turning the page will not create change in and of itself, but it will be a step toward a decision to walk up that steep and rugged ascent toward the light. Prepare to squint, because it is about to get a little brighter.

Twelve

Stronger Than Reality

Throughout the previous chapters, I have made the statement that perception is reality. I need to amend that statement. Perception is actually stronger than reality. If you are looking to quantify how much stronger, it turns out that perception is four times stronger than reality.

In 2011, I conducted a marital satisfaction study that examined the relationship between spirituality, personality, and marital satisfaction[1]. I had grown increasingly disappointed with the limited number of published marital satisfaction research studies that surveyed both the husband and the wife. The vast majority of marital satisfaction research that exists asks individuals about their marriage without also asking their spouses for their input on the same marriage.

I was able to work with 724 individuals, yielding 362 married couples. I was able to ask individuals not only about themselves and their view of their marriage, but also about their spouse. I discovered something very interesting when I asked both husbands and wives to answer the same set of questions about both themselves and their spouse.

Perception is stronger than reality. You may be asking yourself, "What could be stronger than reality; how is that even possible?" Let us take a look, but remember that the purpose of me sharing this with you is to help you out of the metaphorical cave. Although this may help provide answers to some of the stress and tension in your relationship over the past years, our goal here is to influence change upon you and not your spouse. You and your spouse will continue to have differences, but the more you are grounded in reality, the better your chances are of experiencing a thriving marriage and not merely surviving marriage.

Individuals were asked to complete an online questionnaire that included a battery of assessments (RCI-10, FMS, Mini-IPIP, ENRICH 3 Scales, and a demographic survey[2]) that they answered about themselves. As part of the online questionnaire, these same individuals also completed several of the assessments (RCI-10, FMS, Mini-IPIP) answering questions about how they observe their spouse.

The results of the online questionnaire provided me with scores on two spirituality measures and a measure on personality for each spouse. Here is where things began to get interesting, because the questionnaire also provided me observer report ratings for each spouse on both spirituality measures as well as the personality measure. What this meant was that I not only had a score for how each spouse viewed themselves, but I also had the answer for how their spouse viewed them.

I often remind clients that we cannot travel back in time or read minds. Although both would be helpful at times, there are simply some present limitations that we have to work within. But I now had in my hands the next best thing to mind reading. I had 362 husbands telling me what they thought of themselves and what they thought of their wives. I also had 362 wives telling me what they thought of themselves and what they thought of their husbands. I was able to cross reference these objective self reports and observer ratings to see how closely what we think we see matches up with what our spouse believes and sees.

Our Differences

We have all heard the sayings "opposites attract" and "birds of a feather flock together." So which saying is true? It turns out that both sayings contain some truth, but neither is completely accurate when discussing husbands and wives. We tend to marry someone who is similar but not identical to ourselves. American journalist Linda Ellerbee once

> We tend to marry someone who is similar but not identical to ourselves.

noted, "People are pretty much alike. It's only that our differences are more susceptible to definition than our similarities." Our differences can be both the spice of life and the thorn in our side. It has been my experience that when differences pop up unexpectedly, they can cause the most trouble in a marriage, and often times differences pop up unexpectedly because we are either not looking for them or choosing to ignore them in the first place.

The spirituality and marital satisfaction study I conducted found the following: **Similarity between husbands and wives on spirituality measures correlated with marital satisfaction**. What this means is that the more alike you are to your spouse spiritually or religiously speaking, the greater marital satisfaction you reported having. For example, if you like to go to church and your spouse likes to go to church, then that translates into a happier marriage. At the same time, if you do not like going to church and your spouse does not like going to church, that also translated to a happier marriage.

Simply put, the more alike you are, the higher the marital satisfaction scores. In contrast, greater differences between spouses on spirituality correlated to lower marital satisfaction scores. The couples who reported the lowest marital satisfaction scores are the couples in which one spouse scored high on spirituality and was married to an individual who scored low on the same spiritualty measure.

> **What this means is that the more alike you are to your spouse spiritually or religiously speaking, the greater marital satisfaction you reported having.**

The study also found the following to be true: **Higher scores on spirituality measures correlated with higher marital satisfaction scores**. The previous finding focused on how similar you and your spouse are, and this second finding confirmed that the closer you are to God, the more likely you are to have higher marital satisfaction scores. I will admit that it is difficult to measure how close a person is to God.

The measures used in the study assessed both faith maturity and religious commitment, and this combination of faith and actions provided a well-rounded spirituality measure that was correlated to the ENRICH's global marital satisfaction, communication, and conflict resolution scales. The bottom line is that a person's "spirituality" does make a difference in his or her satisfaction with their marriage.

If you are a super-observant reader, you may be wondering already what we could learn if we combined the previous two findings from the study, and that is a great question. Similarity on spirituality correlated with marital satisfaction and levels of spirituality correlated with marital satisfaction, and it was also found that: **Couples who were high on similarity and high on spirituality were those who reported the highest level of marital satisfaction**. Couples who reported the greatest differences on spirituality and the lowest spirituality scores also were those who had the lowest levels of marital satisfaction.

The take away so far could be summarized by saying: Go to church together on Sunday, and as you both draw closer to God, your marriage will benefit from it. Yes, this is an oversimplification of an over-100-page study. I have not even gotten into any of the interesting findings on personality, which may be the single largest predictor of marital satisfaction. The size, scope, and complexity of this study allowed for statistical analysis that has not been possible by any known study to date, which brings us to the really fun stuff.

> Go to church together on Sunday, and as you both draw closer to God, your marriage will benefit from it.

Four Times Greater Than Reality

The findings that have been reported so far are more or less the expected and anticipated results. The correlations I have discussed up until this point have been previously found in other studies or were at least logical hypotheses that had face validity, and I anticipated finding the results that the study produced. It is what I found next that was truly amazing and largely served as the catalyst for this book.

The study examined each spouse's self-report scores on the spirituality measures with their observer-report scores of their spouse. In other words, the study looked at your spirituality and your perception of your spouse's spirituality. There are so few previous studies that captured data from both husband and wife, and no study had ever captured spirituality, personality, and marital satisfaction for married couples. Although I had hypothesized what results may be found, this was uncharted waters. Would it make your marriage any more satisfying if you thought your spouse was more like you, even if it was not true? This is where the contrast between reality and perception has practical applications.

You can answer questions about your faith and your religious commitment, and this becomes a beginning baseline from which to understand your spouse. Your spouse can also answer questions about their faith and religious commitment, and we can then objectively compare and contrast the two responses. On a day-to-day basis, we rarely have a chance to compare your objective self-report against your spouse's objective self-report.

> [I]t turns out that **perception** is **four** times **more powerful** than reality.

What we base most of our decisions and actions upon are our objective self-report (e.g., how we feel, or what we want at any given moment) and our perception of how we believe our spouse would respond (i.e., how we believe they feel or what we believe they want). This may change some day, once we get that mind-reading machine worked out, but until then, husbands and wives are left with what they know of themselves and what they think they know of their spouse.

I anticipated that the study would find that similarity between self-report scores on spirituality and observer-report scores on spirituality would be predictive of marital satisfaction. What I did not anticipate was that the study would find that perceived similarity on spirituality was even more predictive of marital satisfaction than actual similarities on spirituality; in fact, the increase in marital satisfaction scores (over personality correlations alone) was four times greater when correlated with perceived spirituality similarity than with actual spirituality similarity.

The more alike you *think* you are, the greater your marital satisfaction. Throughout the previous chapters, when I made the statement that perception is reality, I could have more accurately said that perception is stronger than reality. And, indeed, it turns out that perception is four times more powerful than reality.

Stepping out of the Cave and into the Light

Some of you may be wondering at this point how closely perception matched reality in the study, and that is a great question. The study found that the way individuals perceive their similarity to their spouse overlaps about 68% with how their spouse viewed themselves. That means our perceptions are skewed by almost a complete one third! This false one third is four times more powerful in predicting our marital satisfaction than reality. Simply stated, individuals are more satisfied with their marriage when they believe that they are similar to their spouse than when they are actually similar to their spouse but do not believe they are.

> Simply stated, individuals are more satisfied with their marriage when they believe that they are similar to their spouse than when they are actually similar to their spouse but do not believe they are.

I warned you in the last chapter that we were going to be stepping out of the cave and seeing our marriage in the bright light of day for the first time. So much of what husbands and wives do in their attempts to survive marriage is almost doomed to fail from the beginning because it is simply not based in reality. When we are happier thinking we are alike than actually being alike, we have some obstacles to overcome.

If our perceptions may be matching reality only two thirds of the time, it is no wonder that couples argue so much. You can begin to see why I said that playing "He Said, She Said" is a fool's errand. He and she aren't even playing on the same game board one third of the time. So, what can be done?

> You can begin to see why I said that playing "He Said, She Said" is a fool's errand. He and she aren't even playing on the same game board one third of the time.

First of all, do not be discouraged. Re-read the previous chapter if you need to, and keep a healthy perspective on what the prisoner was experiencing. Things may appear to get worse before they get better, but they can and will get better. They will get better as long as you do not give up.

If you throw your arms up and say "enough is enough" and run back into the cave and decide to spend the rest of your life staring at shadows, then things will not get any better. I have confidence that just as you have continued to press on in reading this book, you will have the same ability to press on in transforming your marriage through healthy perspectives and more accurate perceptions.

You may be worried that your marriage may be stuck; you have had hope before only to be met with disappointment. While that may be true, you have also had the same limiting perspective and false perceptions through each of those disappointing chapters in your marriage. As you trust that God has your best interest at heart, and as you overcome the discomfort that comes from stepping out of Plato's cave and into the bright sun, you will find that this time will be different than before. Remember, it may appear to get worse before it gets better. But this time you have a fighting chance to make it different as you exploit your new perspectives and let go of some of the perceptions that have failed you before.

Boy Meets Girl

So, let us put all of this research into real-life context and, before we go any further, let us put aside the math, numbers, and statistics for a moment and look at how the connection between perceptions and marital satisfaction looks in the real world. Here is the classic example: Boy meets girl, and boy and girl fall in love—I have run out of pseudonyms, so feel free to use the names of you and your spouse as your read on. Boy and girl go from boyfriend and girlfriend to fiancés. Boy and girl are now husband and wife. Boy has always liked girl, and one of the things that attracted him to her was how spiritually compatible they were.

He would see her at church and they would often discuss what God was doing in the services and what the message meant to them. Fast forward a few months, or years, and girl is less interested in going to church. Boy is shocked, confused, and very concerned and calls a counselor for a marriage counseling appointment. Boy tells the counselor, "She has changed; she used to love going to church but now wants to stay home." Girl replies, "I only went because you liked it. I love God, but I do not need to go to church to have a relationship with God." Girl gets a little flustered as she then adds, "Stop saying that I have changed. I am still the same girl you fell in love with whether I go to church or not."

Perhaps it is not church attendance but something else that has brought a couple in for marriage counseling. Boy meets girl, and boy and girl fall in love; you remember that's how the story starts. When they were dating, girl noticed that boy often had a beer or two when they went out with friends, and although she did not like that boy drank, she dismissed it since it was only a beer or two. Boy, realizing that girl did not drink alcohol, would try to drink no more than two to four beers when they went out with friends.

Several years into marriage, boy's two to four beers is more like four to six and sometimes eight. Boy's drinking has now become a frequent source of contention. Girl is disappointed, confused, and very concerned and calls a counselor for a marriage counseling appointment. Girl tells the counselor, "He has changed."

They've Changed

She/he has changed. That is a phrase that most marriage counselors are familiar with hearing, but it rarely tells the whole story. In both of these examples, they did change, but not as much as the concerned spouse believes. In both examples, the idealistic distortion of the spouse pursuing counseling minimized a difference between the two of them early on in their relationship. Boy believed that girl was more spiritually similar to him than she really was, and girl underestimated

> She/he has changed. That is a phrase that most marriage counselors are familiar with hearing, but it rarely tells the whole story.

boy's affinity for alcohol and how much alcohol he drank. They both saw more of what they wanted to see in their future spouse, and then they were disappointed when one inevitable day they realized that their spouse is not the man or woman they thought they were marrying.

People do change, and in both brief scenarios, the difference between the two spouses grew greater over time. The important difference is that neither spouse changed by as much as the concerned spouse thought they changed.

Some of you reading this book may specifically be frustrated, concerned, or upset by how much your spouse has changed for the worse over the years. It may not be church attendance or drinking beer, but some other area where you believed the two of you were more alike and now you are discovering just how different the two of you

> If greater similarity correlates to greater marital satisfaction, but perceived similarity is a four-times-stronger predictor of marital satisfaction, then we can be at our happiest when we are fooling ourselves.

are. It is often at these moments when one spouse turns to the other and says, "You have changed, you are not the person that I married," that I meet the couple for the first time as they come in for their first marriage counseling session.

If greater similarity correlates to greater marital satisfaction, but perceived similarity is a four-times-stronger predictor of marital satisfaction, then we can be at our happiest when we are fooling ourselves. When we wake up one day and are struck by reality as the carpet of our false perceptions is ripped out from underneath us, our marriage can be threatened.

Our perceptions are stronger than reality, but what if we were able to live in reality? What if we were to take Socrates' word of advice to "[k]now thyself" and also apply them to the one we are married to and "know thy spouse?" Your marriage and your life would dramatically change as you change your perspective and invite your perceptions to more closely match reality. Your foundation for marital satisfaction would be truer, stronger, and more adept at supporting a thriving marriage and not merely surviving marriage.

> Your marriage and your life would dramatically change as you change your perspective and invite your perceptions to more closely match reality.

Over the next several chapters, we are going to walk through several practical steps to bring these philosophical, theoretical, and scientific concepts into the practical day-to-day life of a married couple. The practical tips, tools, and techniques we will discuss will not in and of themselves bring about the meaningful change that your marriage may need. But these tools, coupled with a more complete and accurate perspective that invites healthier perceptions that more closely align with reality, can bring about meaningful change that can transform you from surviving marriage to having a thriving relationship. If you believe you are ready, let us follow the advice of Maria von Trapp and "[s]tart at the very beginning. It's a very good place to start.[3]"

PART IV

BUILDING A THRIVING MARRIAGE

When there is love in a marriage,
there is harmony in the home;

When there is harmony in the home,
there is contentment in the community;

When there is contentment in the community,
there is prosperity in the nation;

When there is prosperity in the nation,
there is peace in the world.

-Chinese Proverb

Thirteen

Ok Smarty Pants, How?

Perspectives inform our perceptions, and our perceptions are the subjective reality that we live in and respond from each and every day. So, if we want to bring about change in our lives, we need to go back to the beginning and change our perspective. Things look different when you are looking at things differently. We cannot sit back and cross our fingers waiting for our spouse to change and expect things to be any better. We can, however, walk around the elephant, change our seat, or walk a mile in our spouse's shoes. Whichever metaphor you prefer at this moment will work just fine, as long as you are willing to take the initiative to see things differently. Since our perspective on things is tied to a literal point of view, if we can gain a new point of view, we will have a different perspective.

Paris-based Swiss artist Felice Varini is famous for his creation of amazing anamorphic illusions[1]. A quick online search will show you just what I mean by amazing. Varini creates unique works of art by superimposing two-dimensional shapes on three-dimensional objects, creating an image that can be seen only when viewed from a certain point of view. When viewed from any other vantage point, all that is seen are random broken geometric shapes. Varini's artwork is a beautiful example of how significant our perspective is in determining what we perceive.

If we want to start building a healthier, stronger,

thriving marriage, we need to begin by looking at things differently. We need a change in our perspective, which means that we first need to be *open* to changing our perspective. As long as we are convinced that the world is flat, or that an elephant is a mighty redwood tree, that will be all that we can see. When we are open to the possibility that what we see may not be all there is, that there may be another side to the story or another way of looking at it, then and only then can true change occur.

You have been patient with this book so far, but by now you may be wanting to know how in the world we go about changing our perspective. It is not like your spouse is an elephant that you can walk around, and my kids frequently walk around the house in my shoes and gain no better understanding of life from my perspective. Metaphors may be helpful in understanding a concept, but let us get to some practical steps to take forward. There is no one special trick or secret intervention that will magically transform your marriage from a surviving marriage to a thriving marriage, and the transformation process will not happen overnight. What we are endeavoring to do is to equip your marriage with the tools that will serve as the building blocks for lasting change.

> It is not like your spouse is an **elephant** that you can walk around, and my kids frequently walk around the house in my shoes and gain no better **understanding** of life from my perspective.

The $64,000 Question

Steve and Beth are the couple we met back in chapter three who "fought every day." When they came in for counseling, I started by laying the same foundation with them that I do with almost every couple or family who presents for counseling: I started by addressing communication. My wife, Jennifer, and I have been teaching a six-week marriage class for the past few years. We begin in session one by addressing communication, and then we warn the couples in the group that we will return to communication in week two and then each and every one of the remaining weeks. Communication is the key to a solid foundation for any healthy relationship.

What is the number-one thing that couples argue about? I will give you a moment in case you want to look it up online, but chances are you do not need to since we discussed it back in chapter nine. Somehow we all seem to be aware that money is the number-one thing that couples argue about. If you take a look at those arguments from a new perspective, it is not truly money that they are arguing over. They argue due to poor communication skills; money just happens to be the context of the poor communication.

> More money rarely solves any real issues within a relationship, but better communication skills often help to avoid many relationship pitfalls before they become issues.

I have worked with couples who, by most standards, are extremely wealthy and yet frequently argued over money. And I have known couples who financially struggle and do not argue over money. What is the difference between couples like these? I would suggest a new perspective that the number-one thing couples argue about is not money but their communication (or lack thereof) over money. How should they spend it? Who makes the decisions on how it comes in and goes out? What does money mean to each spouse? The difference between these couples is not their financial situation but their communication skills.

More money rarely solves any real issues within a relationship, but better communication skills often help to avoid many relationship pitfalls before they become issues. When husbands and wives are on the same page in their relationship, arguments tend to happen far less frequently, but how do you get on the same page with your spouse? That is the $64,000 question[2]. The answer, however, may not cost you any money at all.

Let us back up for one moment. What is communication? Communication involves a message being sent and a message being received. Successful communication requires that the message that is sent matches the message that is received. The best way to broaden your perspective is to successfully communicate with your spouse.

> In order to metaphorically walk around the elephant and see things more completely and more accurately, we need to communicate more effectively.

Award-winning novelist Margaret Millar observed, "Most conversations are simply monologues delivered in the presence of a witness.[3]" Giving a monologue does not equal successful communication; hearing a monologue does not equal successful communication. As Henry David Thoreau articulated, "It takes two to speak the truth,—one to speak, and another to hear.[4]"

It Takes More than Gravity

In order to metaphorically walk around the elephant and see things more completely and more accurately, we need to communicate more effectively. There is no short cut here. Your marriage will not be able to grow stronger than your communication skills.

The more effectively you are able to send a message to your spouse and to have that match the message your spouse receives, the more successfully you will have communicated. The more effectively your spouse is able to send a message to you and to have that match the message you receive, the more successfully you will have communicated. The more effectively you are able to communicate with your spouse, the more success you will have in being able to see things from their perspective.

> As long as we are limited to our old, incomplete, inaccurate perspectives, we are doomed to struggle in attempting to successfully communicate.

Does that sound too simple? Trust me, it is not. If it were easy to communicate more successfully, we would not have so many unhealthy marriages struggling to survive or not surviving at all. What couples often end up with, as children's author and illustrator Robert McCloskey puts it, is "I know you believe you understand what you think I said, but I'm not sure you realize that what you heard is not what I meant.[5]" You may want to read that last sentence a second time to make sure you understand what McCloskey is saying.

As long as we are limited to our old, incomplete, inaccurate perspectives, we are doomed to struggle in attempting to successfully communicate. Carl was stuck with a point of view that there was nothing wrong with hitting things when he got upset. Aleck held to the point of view that it was better to say nothing than to open up with his wife about his true feelings. Amber viewed Brandon's silence as intentional and hurtful. Just as with Steve and Beth, what each of these people needed was a change in perspective that challenged their false perceptions they had accepted as reality.

James L. Framo, in his book *Explorations in Marital & Family Therapy,* explained, "People do not marry people, not real ones anyway; they marry what they think the person is; they marry illusions and images. The exciting adventure of marriage is finding out who the partner really is.[6]" Genuine, effective, and successful communication is the only way we can truly find out who our partner really is.

How many times have you felt that your spouse has not understood you or truly listened to you? I wonder if there is a time that you can recall your spouse listening to you and truly hearing what it is that you were trying to say. If you have ever experienced being heard and understood, then you know what a gift that can be, and it is a gift that you can receive more often. Once again, there are no short cuts here.

Your marriage will not be able to grow stronger than your communication skills. If you desire the gifts that accompany a healthy and thriving marriage, then you are going to need to put in the necessary work. We often hear of couples who fall in love, as if some outside gravitational force pulls them together, but we do not hear of couples who fall into healthy marriages or successful communication patterns. Healthy marriages take work, and to successfully communicate with your spouse takes intentional effort that gravity alone will not produce.

Prince Charming

Many of us grew up dreaming of falling in love with Prince Charming or a beautiful fair maiden, followed by the fairy tale wedding, then the happily ever after. While fairy tales, both before and since Walt Disney's animated adaptations, have not been known for their accurate portrayal of life and love, they do contain some realities that are worth noting.

Cinderella and Prince Charming may have love at first sight, but this is one story that is full of false perception and incomplete realities. Cinderella is not who she pretends to be. While her deception provides possibly the only opportunity for this unlikely couple to have the chance to meet one another, it is also the first obstacle that threatens to destroy their relationship before it even starts.

> We often hear of couples who fall in love, as if some outside **gravitational** force pulls them together, but we do not hear of couples who **fall into** healthy marriages or successful communication patterns.

Snow White also marries a Prince Charming, a young prince who is so enchanted by her beauty as she lays in her coffin that he falls in love with her. The spell is eventually broken, but the young couple in love still has some extended family issues to overcome.

It is Belle and Prince Adam who I believe may have one of the better love stories of all of the fairy tales. They may not have love at first sight, but Belle and Prince Adam certainly demonstrate the hard work that is necessary to make a relationship successful. Better known simply as Beauty and the Beast, this young couple also begin their relationship with incomplete and inaccurate perspectives on each other, but they both work to better understand each other and are able to challenge some false perceptions. You and I may not have singing candlesticks and dancing dishes to help our relationships, but if we are willing to look past what we think we see in order to see what is real and true, we can also overcome some significant communication hurdles.

Belle believes the Beast is, well, a beast, and the Beast believes he will never find true love before his twenty-first birthday. He longs to be loved, but his communication style pushes people away. Through the help of some magical furniture, a wise tea pot, and award-winning music and choreography, Belle and the Beast learn to more effectively communicate. As the story unfolds, we see these two protagonists mature in their ability to express what they want in a healthy and productive way.

I know that I may be a little odd in that, as I watch a movie like Disney's adaptation of *Beauty and the Beast,* I analyze the health of their budding relationship. Perhaps it is in part because my wife and I have three young children, two of whom are girls, whose understanding of love is influenced by the love stories they see in fairy

> You, too, can have your own **happily** ever after.

tales. I suspect it is also the occupational hazard of a counselor, not to mention a preacher forever on the lookout for another good sermon illustration. Nevertheless, the resolve demonstrated by Belle and Prince Adam to overcome their real relationship hurdles can be inspirational for all of us. You, too, can have your own happily ever after.

The good news is that neither you nor your spouse are under the curse of having to find true love by your twenty-first birthday, but the longer you wait to build your happily ever after, the more challenging it will become. So let us jump right into our first exercise designed to improve our communication skills; it is a simple one to understand, but I will admit that it can be challenging to successfully implement when needed most. With some practice, you can learn this new communication skill that will help you look past the Beast in your spouse and see things from his or her perspective. We may not always agree with our spouse, but we can at least seek to understand him or her.

Fourteen

What I Am Hearing You Say Is...

The best way to understand your spouse is to know what they are saying to you. That might sound insultingly simple, but it is a truth far too many married couples overlook. Husbands and wives often miss what their spouse says to them because they are not listening. Ralph Waldo Emerson wrote, "What you do speaks so loudly that I cannot hear what you say.[1]" They may have started off listening, but a few moments into the conversation they shift from listening to what is being said to formulating a response to what they are hearing.

In other words, they shut off their ears so that they can focus on what they are going to say next. This is in part because the human brain can think an estimated 600 to 700 words per minute and the average person only speaks 120 to 150[2]—President John F. Kennedy was known for speaking around 200 words per minute[3]—leaving the mind to wander. Another more germane reason is simply because we are often more interested in what we have to say then what others might be saying to us.

Whatever your motivation and explanation for this bad habit may be, we need to break it. Mohandas (Mahatma) Gandhi said, "Three quarters of the miseries and misunderstandings in the world would finish if people were to put on the shoes of their adversaries and understood their points of view.[4]" You can wear your spouse's shoes all day long, and you will not understand them one ounce better, but what Gandhi and I are suggesting is that you metaphorically step outside of your shoes and pay more attention to the point of view of the one you desire to communicate with. Put on their ears or borrow their eyes; the goal is to expand from your familiar and limited perspective and to see and understand from their point of view. Gandhi's life demonstrated that this technique works even in adversarial relationships.

There is a good chance that you may already be familiar with active listening, but just to ensure that we are all on the same page, allow me to give a brief overview of how I have been using this concept in counseling. The term *active listening* was coined by American clinical psychologist, and colleague of Carl Rogers, Dr. Thomas Gordon. In his book *Leader Effectiveness Training,* Dr. Gordon states, "Active listening is certainly not complex. Listeners need only restate, in their own language, their impression of the expression of the sender. ... Still, learning to do Active Listening well is a rather difficult task ...[5]" Let us focus on the how not complex active listening is first.

Don't Just Listen, Actively Listen

In communication, there are the two parts that we have already discussed: a message sent and a message received. Active listening focuses on the messaged received, but we will get back to the message sent in the next chapter. Active listening requires you to:

- Listen to what the speaker is speaking to you verbally
- Observe what the speaker is communicating to you nonverbally
- Organize and summarize what you have perceived that they have shared with you

- Paraphrase back to the speaker what you have heard them say

Basically you are being asked to listen and reflect back what you have heard them say to you—certainly not that complex. I give listeners a few more pointers or tips that I would also encourage you to follow if you are new to active listening, or if you have unsuccessfully tried it in the past:

- Before you respond, look your spouse in the eyes
- Begin your response by speaking their name
- Use the phrase "what I am hearing you say is"
- Include a feeling or emotion word in your response

Looking your spouse in the eyes creates an intimate connection and helps the two of you focus in on what is being said. There is a power in knowing and speaking a person's name. Anthony Bloom wrote, "A relationship becomes personal and real the moment you begin to single out a person from the crowd.[6]" Looking your spouse in the eye and then speaking his or her name singles out your spouse from everyone else competing for your attention, even if you are all alone in a room.

> Looking your spouse in the eye and then speaking his or her name singles out your spouse from everyone else competing for your attention

The goal of this exercise is to do more than just confirm that you have heard your spouse correctly, but to strengthen and deepen your relationship. When was the last time you truly looked your spouse in the eyes while talking? Our eyes are often distracted by our smart phones, the television, or what the kids are doing in the background, and we miss the gift we can give and receive by making genuine eye contact with our spouse while talking with them.

I like to encourage couples to then use the phrase "what I am hearing you say is" as they begin to respond to their spouse for a few reasons. I realize this is not normal human behavior. Back when I was an undergraduate student in Bible College, my Psychology 101 professor had us practice active listening over the weekend as a homework assignment. My wife had no idea what I was doing and it sort of freaked her out at first, but she had never felt more heard before in her life.

Beginning with the phrase "what I am hearing you say is" initially serves as a code between you and your spouse that you are trying to summarize and confirm that you have heard what they have intended to say. The phrase communicates to your spouse that you are taking a sidebar from the conversation at hand to verify that the two of you are still on the same page before proceeding any further.

The choice of words in the phrase is intentional, too. We are not saying "this is what you have said," but instead quite literally "this is what I am hearing you say." This allows you, as the active listener, to take the responsibility for any misunderstanding or misinterpretation of what was said. You are tentatively offering a summary of what you think was said. This subtle difference may help diffuse an argument that could arise if your spouse perceives that you are throwing words back in his or her face. You are not telling your spouse what he or she said; you are telling him or her what you have heard. In a moment, you are going to look for feedback at how well you did and if your spouse felt that you accurately understood the message.

Feeling, Nothing More Than Feelings

There is at least one more component to our reflection that is critically important. When we are reflecting back to our spouse what we have heard them say, we should also include a feeling or emotion word. It is helpful if our spouse uses a feeling or emotion word when they are sharing, but even when they do not, there was likely an emotion that was being conveyed.

You, as the listener, may have to think about this for a moment, but internally you are processing the message and you are sensing a feeling even if you struggle to name it. If you simply paraphrase what you have heard your spouse say, but neglect the emotion, you may then be ascribing a different meaning to what was said than what he or she had meant to convey to you. Our goal is to change our perspective from what we are seeing and hearing and to expand that perspective to include what our spouse is attempting to communicate.

> Our goal is to change our perspective from what we are seeing and hearing and to expand that perspective to include what our spouse is attempting to communicate.

If you want to walk a mile in your spouse's shoes, you need to get out of your own and immerse yourself in your spouse's shoes. We are not mind readers, so we must rely on feedback from our spouse as to whether or not we have accurately received their message. The total message includes both verbal and nonverbal communication as well as the facts and the emotions being conveyed.

Let us look at the following example from Brandon and Amber:

[Amber] Honey, our anniversary is coming up next week, and I would really like to do something nice. It would make me feel very special if you would surprise me and plan the evening out.

[Brandon] Amber, what I am hearing you say is that you would like me to plan our anniversary this year. It would make you feel very special if I surprised you with a fancy night out on the town and you did not have to do any of the planning this year.

Brandon did a nice job summarizing and paraphrasing what he was hearing Amber say. Amber was helpful enough to share that she would feel "very special" if Brandon did what she was asking. Brandon may have perceived that the anniversary plans were a burden to Amber and could have reflected back that Amber would feel "relieved," which may or may not have been accurate. Brandon did hear Amber say "something really nice"

> Even when you accurately hear the words that they say, there is still room for communication error.

and interpreted that to mean "fancy night out on the town," which again may or may not have been what Amber meant by "really nice." By reflecting back what we have heard through active listening, we then have an opportunity to check in with our spouse and see just how close our perception of the conversation matches what our spouse intended to communicate.

I cannot emphasize enough how important it is to discover what your spouse is attempting to communicate to you and for you not to assume based on what you heard them say that your perception of what they said matches the reality of what they meant. Even when you accurately hear the words that they say, there is still room for communication error.

Just the other day, I was meeting with a young man who said that he loves his girlfriend. They had recently broken up, so ex-girlfriend may be a more accurate description, but with their on-again, off-again relationship and three children together, he still considers her his girlfriend and is telling me he loves her. I asked the young man what he meant by saying he loves her. He admitted to me that he did not quite understand my question.

I said to him, "I know what the Bible says love is, I know what the dictionary says love is, but I do not know what you believe love is." As it turns out, he did not know what love is. He shared with me how deep his feelings are for her and that every night since she left him three months ago, he has gotten drunk to the point

> Even if you are not going to come to an agreement with your spouse on what love is, you need to at least begin with understanding what they mean by the word when they use it when communicating with you.

of blacking out. He recounted their tormented years together characterized by arguments, hostility, aggression, and unforgiveness, and believed he loved her since he is now so depressed and miserable living alone.

As I listened intently to this young man, actively listened, I was able to pick up on the discrepancy between what I was hearing him say and what I believed I was hearing him say. We processed the incongruence, and it helped both of us better understand what was being said.

What Active Listening Is Not

While we are on the topic of love, in *The Discipline of Grace,* Jerry Bridges offers that "[l]ove is essentially a motive. Someone has made the point that love is a verb...it is true that love is a verb, not a feeling...In another sense, however, love is not a verb but the motive that prompts and guides other verbs: that is, certain actions.[7]" Jerry Bridges gives the example that he can love his enemies by forgiving them for their harmful actions toward him and then seeking their welfare in appropriate ways, and he then points out that the verbs in his example are *forgive* and *seek*. He then comes to the conclusion that "[l]ove always needs other verbs to give it hands and feet. By itself it can do nothing."

Suffice it to say that there are a lot of competing and sometimes contradictory definitions and understandings of what love is. Even if you are not going to come to an agreement with your spouse on what love is, you need to at least begin with understanding what they mean by the word when they use it when communicating with you.

Here are a few other noteworthy points about active listening before we turn to the message-sending half of communication. When reflecting back, the listener is:

- Not stating that they agree with the speaker
- Not saying that they will do what the speaker is requesting
- Not defending any perceived accusations
- Not trying to solve any problems
- Not formulating a response
- Waiting to hear back from the speaker if they have heard them correctly or not

The purpose of active listening and the reflection back is to engage you, as the listener, into the communication process more effectively. John Marshall, arguably the most influential Chief Justice of the Supreme Court our country has ever had, once said, "To listen well is as powerful a means of communication and influence as to talk well.[8"] Listening is often considered something passively done by the listener, but when we passively listen, we are not fully utilizing all that God has gifted us with.

Active listening engages listeners more strategically so that they can maximize a communication exchange, but remember that we are still listening. We have failed as a good listener if we are thinking of what we are going to say in response instead of first hearing what has been said. I know it can be frustrating going to doctors when they give you a diagnosis before hearing all of your symptoms. Even if their diagnosis is correct, there is a comfort that comes from knowing that you have been heard or at least given a chance to share. That comfort that comes with knowing that you have been heard helps you to become more engaged in the process.

> We have failed as a good listener if we are thinking of what we are going to say in response instead of first hearing what has been said.

Transitioning from you and your spouse surviving marriage to experiencing a thriving marriage will require both of you to truly be engaged in the process. Listen to your spouse, practice active listening, and watch what happens. You can thank me later.

Active listening takes practice, and a lot of it. You are essentially retraining yourself on a skill you learned in infancy. As an infant, you communicated (i.e., screamed, cried) because you wanted something, but as adults in a marriage relationship, we ought to be using communication more effectively. Remember, we are talking about active listening at this point as a tool to help us extend beyond our own limited and potentially inaccurate perspective in order

THE ELEPHANT IN THE MARRIAGE

to see things better from the perspective of our spouse.

Our perspectives inform our perceptions, and our perceptions are greater than reality. By getting a window into our spouse's perspective, we are given a glimpse of their reality. This peek at the world through their eyes is not quite mind reading, but it is possibly the best non-science-fiction runner up.

> Our perspectives inform our perceptions, and our perceptions are greater than reality.

Fifteen

How Can They Hear
without Someone Speaking?

The previous chapter may be helpful when you are the listener, but what do you do with the other half of the time when you are the one speaking? I am so glad you asked! There are several things that you can do as the one in the relationship doing the talking, and the first thing is to do some talking. This is often referenced in communication literature as assertiveness.

We have already established the fact that as the listener, you cannot read minds. Guess what? Your spouse cannot read your mind either. If there is something that you want, you need to ask for it. If there is something that you do not like, you need to share that with your spouse. If there is something that is on your mind, it will stay there until you put your thoughts to words and communicate it to your spouse.

I know that growing up in the church, I was taught that the meek shall inherit the earth (Matthew 5:5), and I grew up viewing assertiveness akin to being a bully and potentially sinful. Some may hold a similar concern and a view that it is virtuous to not speak your mind, to not request what you would like, to not share your likes and dislikes, and to just attempt to please those around you.

When you couple the Sermon on the Mount with Jesus' teaching on the first shall be last and the last shall be first

(Matthew 20:16), you could easily believe the notion that you are helping your marriage by keeping your wants, desires, hopes, and dreams locked up inside. This behavior reminds me of something C.S. Lewis wrote: "Human Beings all over the earth have this curious idea that they ought to behave in a certain way, and they can't really get rid of it.[1]" Let us see if we can get rid of *this* curious idea of how we ought to behave and infuse some health in the way we choose to communicate with our spouse.

We have already explored how communication requires a message sent and a message received, and in the previous chapter we focused on how you can better receive the messages sent by your spouse. For the health of your relationship, you also need to learn how to better send your message. This is not about being selfish, getting your way, or taking control, but it is about empowering your spouse to love you better by understanding you better. When communicating with your spouse, try to remember the following suggestions:

- Make eye contact.
- Begin by using your spouse's name.
- Speak using "I" statements.
- Incorporate an emotion or feeling word.
- Cut down your monologue to manageable portions. (think tweet, not blog post)

The first two suggestions ought to look familiar from the previous chapter, but they both serve an additional purpose when you are the one communicating the message by helping to ensure that your spouse is listening. Our example earlier of Brandon and Amber in chapter ten would have gone completely differently if Amber first ensured that she had the attention of Brandon. So many relationship arguments have their root in the "I told you/No you didn't" cycle.

Over 300 years ago, the question was first posed, "If a tree falls in a forest and no one is around to hear it, does it make a sound?[2]" Husbands and wives have been debating a similar question for many more centuries: "If you were told something and you did not hear it, were you told anything?"

Making eye contact and addressing your spouse, either by given name or a loving nickname, increases the odds that he or she is actually listening to you. Amber perceived that Brandon was ignoring her; at least that is how she saw it from her perspective. Brandon was simply engaged elsewhere and did not hear his wife's

> **If you were told something and you did not hear it, were you told anything?**

question. This happens more frequently than we realize, and the result is that spouses neglect to remember a doctor's appointment, forget that a friend was going out of town, or never get around to signing a permission slip. Also possible is that your spouse never heard you mention the doctor's appointment, the mutual friend heading out of town, and the permission slip. Perception is greater than reality, so let us try getting on the same page with our spouse and share some overlapping reality.

There's No "I" in Team, but
There Is One in Communication

Speaking using "I" statements is not about being self-centered or making it all about you. Quite the contrary, speaking to your spouse using "I" statements is a technique that can help your spouse hear and receive more of what you are communicating to them. Shifting to using more "I" statements can be a bit challenging initially, but your spouse will greatly appreciate it. Using "I" statements is largely about you, the speaker, taking ownership and responsibility for what you are speaking instead of displacing the responsibility onto your listener. Here is a cliché example of what not to do:

"*Brandon, you always leave your socks on the floor!*"

There are so many ways to improve that attempt to communicate. Let us give Amber credit for at least beginning by speaking her husband's name, even if she was potentially yelling or speaking in anger. When Brandon is hearing this accusation, he may immediately feel attacked. When we are attacked, a natural response is to put up our defenses, which often ironically includes putting up an emotional or mental wall for protection, and we shut down, withdraw, or stop listening. Amber's attempt to communicate something to Brandon prompts Brandon to block out what Amber is attempting to say.

> Perception is greater than reality, so let us try getting on the same page with our spouse and share some overlapping reality.

An alternative and potentially more productive approach would be for Amber to reconstruct her message by shifting from a "you" statement to an "I" statement. Let us also go ahead and incorporate an emotion or feeling word, like we discussed in the previous chapter, and then rephrase Amber's message:

"*Brandon, when I see socks on the bedroom floor, I feel disrespected. I would like to be able to come home from work and find the bedroom at least as clean as when I left for the office in the morning.*"

Brandon is far more likely to hear and receive Amber's message when it is presented in a less hostile manner. Even if Amber's first attempt is offered in a calm voice, it still comes across as an accusation. In Amber's second attempt, her use of "I" statements allows her to take ownership of what is being communicated. She is still saying that she does not like socks on the floor, but the focus is on her. Amber's second attempt is less likely to trigger Bandon's emotional defenses, and the odds are increased that he will be able to hear Amber's message. Using "I" statements shifts the goal of communication from merely letting off steam, like in the first example, to helping your spouse understand something from your perspective so that you may be able to work toward a resolution.

Brandon has also now heard how Amber feels when she sees socks on the floor, and the bedroom floor in particular. This emotional component adds important information above and beyond the mere accusation in Amber's first attempt. And since emotions are an important component of communication— coupled with the findings that more of our message is communicated nonverbally than verbally—Thomas Gordon advises that there should be congruence between the words spoken and the speaker's affect, tone of voice, facial expressions, and body language[3]. Our goal is to communicate a message to our spouse, and not to confuse them with mixed messages. If our body language speaks more loudly than our spoken words, the nonverbal communication may be the one and only message they receive.

> If our body language speaks more loudly than our spoken words, the nonverbal communication may be the one and only message they receive.

Never Say Never

May I also suggest deleting a few words from your vocabulary?

- Always
- Never
- Every time

Okay, maybe you do not need to completely remove them from your vocabulary, but let us try to give them a rest, become aware of how often we use them, and take a break from using them for a few months. I am sure that Brandon does not *always* leave his socks on the floor. Brandon is aware that he does not *always* leave his socks on the floor. Brandon could easily, and naturally defensively, respond to Amber's accusation that he *always* leaves his socks on the floor by saying that he does not *always* leave his socks on the floor.

Brandon could recall a time, perhaps six or seven months ago, that he had stepped in a large puddle and his socks became so wet that he draped his dripping socks over the couch so that they could dry out. He does not *always* leave his socks on the floor. Amber would not likely be impressed with the one time Brandon recalls not leaving his socks on the floor, and they may either shift to arguing over the word *always* or escalate to a full-blown argument.

> The truth is that rarely does someone do something always, or never, or every time.

The truth is that rarely does someone do something always, or never, or every time. Using one of those words for added emphasis shifts a potentially accurate statement to an inflammatory statement, which then only causes your listener to get defensive. Defensiveness reduces receptiveness. Reduced receptiveness increases hostility. Increased hostility leads to fighting or other damaging behaviors. There does not appear to be much good that comes from using always, never, and every time, and there does seem to be some damaging effects. I will suggest one more time that we give those words a rest in our conversations with our spouse. After all, if we are saying something that is not true, we call that lying. Lying to your spouse rarely serves as a good foundation for communication.

Instead, we may need to say what we mean and mean what we say. As the originator of the message, you have the responsibility of effectively communicating a message to your spouse. Say what you mean, and mean what you say. Your spouse cannot read your mind, nor should they have to; be honest with them. If you do not want any gifts for your birthday, then say so. However, if you do want a gift for your birthday, do not lie and deceive by saying that you will be okay if you do not get any gifts this year. Say what you mean, and mean what you say. How else is your spouse going to learn to trust and understand you?

In Real Time

This might require us to do some soul searching first. If we do not know what we want, how in the world can we ever expect that our spouse would know? It is unfair to your spouse and destructive to your relationship to expect something of your spouse that you have not invested the time and energy in figuring out for yourself. This shift in perspective alone will pay back amazing dividends. Take the time to discover what respect, love, encouragement, and joy mean to you, and then communicate these understandings to your spouse. You will then be better empowered to say what you mean and mean what you say because you will know what it is that you would like to say.

Saying what you mean and meaning what you say will also help with the congruence between your verbal and nonverbal communication. Sending mixed messages truly takes a toll on your relationship. It can leave your spouse second guessing and running around in circles. I often encourage people to take their spouse at their word, even if they believe that their spouse does not mean them. This can be a tough exercise, but the goal is to break some of the destructive negative communication cycles.

> Sending mixed messages truly takes a toll on your relationship.

This is similar to those who set all of their clocks in the house 15 minutes fast so that they trick themselves into thinking that they are late. What happens when they encounter a clock with the real time or a clock that is slow or even faster? I prefer to have all of the clocks in our house say what they mean and mean what they say. It is then my responsibility to respond to the truth.

Pulling many of these communication skills together introduces a different culture with your spouse, and this is where you really begin to see some great things occur. If you are the one sending the message, be mindful of the message that is being sent. When you are the one receiving the message, actively listen and reflect back what you are hearing. Over the course of communication, you will alternate roles with your spouse, taking turns as both the listener and the speaker.

Give special attention to the role that you are in, taking personal responsibility to do your very best, and in time you will notice an improvement in your communication skills. The better you are able to communicate, the more you will be empowered to better understand your spouse's perspective. Understanding your spouse's perspective will help expand or correct your perspective, which will in turn challenge or shape your perceptions. Communication is key, and you will see how each of the next chapters builds upon the communication skills presented in this and the previous chapter.

Sixteen

It May Take Two to Tango, But Only One to Change Your Marriage

L et us be honest, marriage counseling works best when both the husband and the wife are engaged in seeking God's best for their marriage. I know that when I have a husband and wife coming in for counseling, and they are both invested in and committed to the process, God can and does do some truly amazing things. This chapter is aimed at all of the spouses who perceive that they are unable to convince their husband or wife to give counseling a try.

While I may not know you and what your spouse is or is not willing to do, I sincerely and wholeheartedly believe that powerful and meaningful changes can be made as long as there is one spouse who is willing to do some work. It takes one spouse willing to fight for a marriage, and to not give up when the going gets tough.

The going will get tough. As human beings, we naturally enjoy receiving some positive feedback when we invest energy into our marriage. When we take out the trash, we may look for a thank you. When we prepare a nice dinner, we may look for a compliment. When we go out of our way to do something for our spouse, we naturally would like some sort of acknowledgement that the effort was noticed and appreciated.

In a healthy and thriving marriage, these positive feedback loops are present and to be expected. In less than healthy or dysfunctional marriages, we may need to think about receiving a thank you or an acknowledgement as a goal rather than an expectation. If your spouse is not willing or able to partner with you through the process of improving your marriage, it may literally take you making a decision to fight for your marriage.

As long as you are willing to selflessly invest the blood, sweat, time, and tears into the marriage, there is hope that a healthier marriage is possible. In this chapter, I would like to give you a few practical weapons to help you fight for your marriage, but many of them will work only in conjunction with the proper perspective.

I had a client once tell me that he would be willing to do anything for his marriage, to which I replied, "I have seen God do some amazing things as long as one spouse is willing to fight for the marriage." My client responded that he would do whatever it took, as long as it took, to fight for his marriage, but then he added, "as long as my wife does her part, too." I told him, and now you, that it does not work that way.

> You cannot say in one breath that you are willing to do whatever it takes, but then in the next breath say you will keep trying only if you see your spouse working hard, too.

You cannot say in one breath that you are willing to do whatever it takes, but then in the next breath say you will keep trying only if you see your spouse working hard, too. Your spouse may not see the value of marriage counseling; make marriage counseling a goal then, rather than a starting point. Remember, while easier with two, it takes only one to change a marriage. If you are going to be the one fighting for your marriage, review the pre-change steps discussed in chapter three, and keep these thoughts in mind:

- Lead your heart; do not be led by your heart.
- Do not anticipate or expect positive feedback for your efforts.
- Focus proactively on your Circle of Influence rather than reactively on your Circle of Concern.
- Be the change you want to see in your marriage.
- Any victories will come from God and not from you.

Take the Lead

Let us begin with leading your heart. Although not a new concept, I appreciate the way that Stephen and Alex Kendrick begin their book *The Love Dare* by saying, "The world says to follow your heart, but if you are not leading it, then someone or something else is...We dare you to think differently—choosing instead to *lead your heart* toward that which is best in the long run.[1]"

When fighting for your marriage, you will feel the ups and downs of the daily victories and defeats; if you allow your heart to dictate what kind of day it is

> Growth, change, and health take intentionality that needs to be sustained over the long haul and not based upon what our hearts may feel at any given moment.

going to be, then you and your spouse will likely spend your time spinning your wheels and hurting each other in the process. Growth, change, and health take intentionality that needs to be sustained over the long haul and not based upon what our hearts may feel at any given moment.

When we decide to lead our heart, we preemptively and

proactively take responsibility for our actions and our emotions. Leading our heart invites us to make healthier decisions for our relationship because our decisions can be more intentional and less reactive. Fighting for your marriage will take sustained effort over an extended period of time, and success in fighting toward a healthy relationship will be undermined by unproductive behaviors.

Remember, perspectives inform our perceptions, and our perceptions are stronger than reality. When introducing healthy change into the relationship, realities need to be altered in order to reap the full benefits of the change. If your spouse believes that you are still the same, then your efforts will go unnoticed or may be discounted. You may need to invest prolonged energy into leading your heart until your spouse's perceptions of you are challenged and he or she is open to accepting a new reality.

You may have a history of being emotionally distant from your spouse, and you are now making the conscious decision to be more emotionally engaged. You have decided to lead your heart instead of being led by your heart. On your way home from work, you cling to the steering wheel and reflect on the day, struggling to answer the question, "How was your day, hon?" You honestly do not know, but you do know that your spouse wants to hear how your day was, and that means feelings and details.

> You may need to invest prolonged energy into leading your heart until your spouse's perceptions of you are challenged and he or she is open to accepting a new reality.

You mentally relive the day as you sit in gridlock, grateful for the extra time to figure out how you felt throughout the day. When you finally arrive home and see your spouse, you are prepared to respond to the daily inquiry. Weeks go by and you are getting much better at sharing how your day was, and although your spouse has yet to make a single encouraging comment, you know that you are making significant progress.

Then one day, you just have a really rough day, and you spend the car ride home not wanting to relive another single moment. You walk in the door, and when asked about your day, you stonewall. You do not want to unleash your anger over how the day was, and you simply choose not to talk about it.

Your spouse's perception of you is once again reinforced, and he or she starts right back where you left off weeks ago and says, "You are always so emotionally distant, and you never tell me how your day was." Perhaps your spouse has learned to remove *always* and *never* from his or her vocabulary and instead replies, "I knew you hadn't truly changed; you are the same person I married, and you just aren't capable of sharing your emotions with me."

It is at moments like this when fighting for our marriage becomes critical as we decide to lead our heart and continue to fight for change. If we are dependent upon positive reinforcement for our efforts or give up when our efforts are dismissed, then we are being led by our heart. To paraphrase Mohandas (Mahatma) Gandhi, "Be the change you want to see in your marriage,[2]" and proactively change the culture in your marriage.

> Stop worrying about things that you cannot change, and direct your efforts toward those things that you can change for the better.

Stop worrying about things that you cannot change (how your spouse will respond), and direct your efforts toward those things that you can change for the better (your actions).

Stephen Covey famously described this effort as focusing more on your Circle of Influence and less on your Circle of Concern[3]. There are things that we can be concerned about, but we have very little or no influence over changing them. Stop worrying about them. Instead, focus your energy on your smaller Circle of Influence, and you will find yourself far more effective in your efforts. What you will also find is that your Circle of Influence will increase as you earn the opportunity to positively influence more of the things that you are concerned about.

Thirty Seconds to a Better Marriage

Worrying about things in and of itself does not bring about any productive change. What if we were able to shift our energy from ruminating to praying? Prayer has the powerful ability to change things, including those praying. I love how pastor and author Rod Loy puts it: "We're active partners in the process. But make no mistake: We're *junior* partners.[4]" You may already be praying for your spouse, but when was the last time that you prayed with your spouse?

I am not talking about an all-night prayer rally or even an extended time around the church altars, but when was the last time that you joined hands with your spouse or even laid your hand on your spouse's shoulder and prayed for anything other than the meal that was before you? If you believe, as I do, that there is power in prayer and that prayers change things, why would we not use one of the best marital aids available?

Saint Augustine is often quoted as saying, "Pray as though everything depended on God. Work as though everything depended on you.[5]" Here is a chance for you to work on your marriage through prayer in as little as thirty seconds a day. You may scoff at the idea of praying for as little as thirty seconds. If you are praying with your spouse already for longer than thirty seconds a day, then feel free to skip ahead, but if you cannot recall the last time you have prayed with your spouse, then thirty seconds may be just the right size.

- Decide upon a time of day that may be the most successful.
- Ask your spouse if there is something that you could pray about for them.
- Keep the prayer short, simple, and focused.
- The goal is thirty seconds.
- This is not a time to plead your case before God over an issue you are arguing about.
- This is a time to invite God into your marriage through prayer.
- Aim to pray on more days than not.
- As you become more successful, aim to pray almost everyday.

Be willing to be the only one who prays, but be prepared with a prayer request should your spouse ask you what he or she can pray about for you. We are not looking to make your time of prayer yet another thing to argue over, so be mindful to lead your heart through this experiment. The presence of God changes lives, and if you can invite the presence of God into your marriage, significant and meaningful change is possible.

> The presence of God changes lives, and if you can invite the presence of God into your marriage, significant and meaningful change is possible.

Imagine if you were willing to stop and interrupt a day

where you and your spouse were struggling relationally to pray. If your heart was right and your motives were pure, your prayer would help to interrupt an ongoing negative cycle. The content of your prayer and the invitation for God to move in your relationship have the potential to alter the trajectory of your day and to bring the two of you to a place that might not have otherwise been possible.

The goal is not to be perfect, but to consistently create space for God in your marriage. Rarely have I encountered anyone who has not been open to accepting a prayer, if they sense that your motives are genuine. Protect these thirty seconds of prayer from any temptation to passively-aggressively communicate anything to your spouse. If you need to say something to your spouse, say it to your spouse. When you want to pray for your spouse, pray for your spouse. When you confuse the two, you taint the precious gift that prayer can be for your relationship.

Deposits of Love

Allow prayer to be added to your repertoire of tangible expressions of love that can make deposits into your spouse's love bank. The term *love bank* has been used by so many in varying ways, so allow me to clarify what I mean by love bank as it relates to your marriage. You may find it helpful to conceptualize your interactions with your spouse as a series of deposits and withdrawals from a metaphorical *love bank*.

When you make your spouse breakfast, you make a small deposit; make them breakfast in bed, and you may be making a slightly larger deposit. Come home late for dinner, and you make a withdrawal; come home late for your anniversary dinner, and you make a much larger withdrawal. You may not be able to go to the ATM to check your current balance, but trust me, your relationship keeps a running tally, and at any given time your *love bank* has either a balance or a deficit.

Your relationship requires regular and ongoing deposits in order to maintain a healthy balance. Introducing the thirty-second prayer may be one such deposit. You should not treat your spouse's love bank like paying taxes to the Internal Revenue Service, trying to figure out what the minimum is that can be given to stay out of trouble. You need to lead your heart, fight for your marriage, and take the responsibility to overwhelmingly bless your spouse with deposits, as many and as large as you can imagine.

> Your relationship requires regular and ongoing deposits in order to maintain a healthy balance.

This is where it takes some intentionality and some creativity. We live in the real world, and there are time and financial restrictions on what can be done, but a shift in perspective toward looking for ways you can bless your spouse through frequent and meaningful deposits can help your spouse feel like richest person in the world.

There is also a real possibility that you find that your spouse's love bank is in the red and has been running a negative balance for a while. Imagine that your real-life checking account is $5,000 in the negative, and you make a $100 deposit. Your account is still overdrawn, and you still have no positive balance from which to cover new charges. You could continue to make $100 deposits each and every week for an entire year, but when you factor in overdraft fees and bounced check fees, you will still be below zero until the day comes when you have consistently and intentionally deposited enough to celebrate being broke, dead even, and penniless.

Imagine that your spouse has a *love bank,* and your relationship has a *love bank,* and they are both lacking any positive funds. Do not give up, continue to make deposits, and approach your relationship as you would your bank account. You cannot anticipate that a bank will be glad to let you spend money just because you are less in debt than you used to be. You have to be generous with your deposits and extremely careful with your withdrawals.

> You cannot anticipate that a bank will be glad to let you spend money just because you are less in debt than you used to be.

John Gottman's research into marital stability has found that relationships that have a five-to-one ratio of positive interactions to negative interactions are more likely to be stable relationships that last[6]. This roughly translates into five deposits into your spouse's *love bank* for any withdrawals, assuming that there is already a balance to cover the withdrawal. I know that this can sound like a lot of work, and as I said earlier in this chapter, marriage counseling works best when both the husband and wife are engaged in seeking God's best for the marriage, but take hope that even if your spouse is not at a place to help fight for the marriage, you can still see powerful and meaningful change.

> [Y]ou plus God is always a majority

Mark Batterson, in his best-selling book *The Circle Maker*, challenges us with this truth, "Most of us don't get what we want because we quit praying. We give up too easily. We give up too soon. We quit praying right before the miracle happens.[7]" Do not give up: Continue creating space for God to have victories and to do the miraculous and impossible. It is you and God working together, and to paraphrase Frederick Douglass, you plus God is always a majority[8].

Seventeen

Give Voice to the Couple

It took me months to purchase my last couch. When I was voted in as the lead pastor of a church south of Washington, D.C., there was already a couch in that office. Years later, when I accepted the position of Care Pastor at another church, I found myself in need of purchasing a new couch. There may not be too many things that a person expects to find when entering a counselor's office, but a couch is generally one of them.

My couch was one of the things that distinguished my office from all of the other offices in the church's administrative wing. I wanted a black leather couch that was comfortable, but not too comfy. I was looking for a couch that would be just the right size—not too big for my office, but certainly not one that looked undersized. Most important, the couch had to have three cushions. Whenever I meet with a new couple for marriage counseling, I mention the couch and explain that it has three cushions on purpose. I explain that one cushion is for the husband, one cushion is for the wife, and the third cushion is for my client, the couple (i.e., marriage, relationship).

People can tend to be self-centered by nature, and by that I simply mean that they naturally see the world from their own perspective. When we get married, we take on the challenge of making an intentional effort to see the world from our spouse's perspective; while this can be both challenging and beneficial, it still remains insufficient.

Husbands and wives who desire more than merely surviving marriage need to learn to view the world through a third and less-intuitive perspective. In order to experience a thriving marriage, couples must develop the ability to see from the perspective of the relationship and give a voice to the couple itself.

The standard marriage advice for generations has been to seek a compromise, some sort of halfway point between what the husband and wife each desire. While there may be limited times that this simple approach can work, a far more successful, even if more challenging, approach is to ask what is best for the relationship and to inquire of the marriage what it wants.

Trust me, the marriage has hopes and desires just as much as the husband and wife do individually, but if we never ask the relationship what it wants, we may never find out. In order for you and your spouse to experience a thriving marriage, you will need to be open to broadening your perspective and seeing things through the eyes and ears of your marriage. This new perspective will alter some of the perceptions you have held onto in the past and help create a new reality for you, your spouse, and your marriage.

> Trust me, the marriage has hopes and desires just as much as the husband and wife do individually…

The evolution of the standard marriage advice to seek a compromise was to seek win-win outcomes. When a couple aims to find a win-win outcome, they are not merely trying to meet in the middle and compromise where neither the husband nor the wife truly get what they want, but instead they are creatively trying to find a solution where both the husband and the wife each are able to get what they want.

This is better but not good enough to thrive.

What happens when the husband and wife each get what they want but neither considers the relationship? When you give voice to the couple, your perspective shifts, and you begin considering win-win-win outcomes. There may also be times when the husband and wife may each knowingly chose a lose-lose in order for the marriage to receive the win.

A Winning Relationship

I realize that each couple is unique, and what is a win for one person or one couple might not be considered a win for another, but let me illustrate a few real-life examples:

- Husband and wife consistently choose to separate for the holidays so that they can each be with their families, but this never allows the two of them to enjoy a major holiday together.
- Husband wants to golf and wife wants to ski, so they take separate vacations.
- Husband and wife cannot agree on how to handle the family finances, so they decide to keep their own paychecks and do their finances separately, just as they did when they were single.
- Husband and wife both have demanding work schedules, long for companionship, and often enjoy the company of the opposite gender for late dinners.
- One spouse sees that the other has spent money on him- or herself, so the spouse does likewise. In return, the other spouse spends money on him- or herself again, and the other again does likewise.
- One spouse is a night owl and the other an early riser, so they go to bed separately and wake up on different schedules, leaving little time throughout the week to see each other.

- Husband and wife get into an argument, and each believes that he or she is owed an apology and waits to apologize until receiving an apology first.

You might take offense at one or more of these examples, and perhaps you may be able to offer some better illustrations, but the point here is that even if you get what you want, you still lose if the relationship does not win. Your relationship is a living and breathing entity that not only deserves its own cushion on my couch, but also needs to have its voice heard, to have someone standing up for its best interests. The only way for you to truly win is for your relationship to win.

> **The only way for you to truly win is for your relationship to win.**

Rules of Engagement

If you have seen the movie *A Beautiful Mind,* perhaps you recognize this idea from the theory that earned John Nash a Nobel Prize in Economics[1]. John Nash recognized the shortcoming of the "everyman for himself" mindset and suggested the best results come from everyone in the group doing what is best for themselves and the group. Thinking of others and not being selfish may have come as a revolutionary idea to the world of economics, but the Word of God has been teaching these principles for millennia. Husbands and wives would do well to truly practice what Christ taught in Luke 6:31, "Do to others as you would have them do to you." Remembering the Golden Rule and applying it to your marriage is one way to not only bless your spouse, but also protect and give voice to your relationship.

More than a cushion to sit on, the relationship needs active consideration in how you and your spouse interact.

Thinking of your spouse first when life is going well and the relationship is healthy is important, but being able to do so when there is tension or conflict is crucial to the health of any relationship. Husbands and wives can prevent a lot of heartache and damage to the marriage if they learn to fight differently. The Geneva Convention treaties, ratified by 196 countries in 1949, outline how we are allowed to fight with one another as sovereign nations. Think about that for just a moment: We have international rules that dictate how we are allowed to attack and kill our enemies. Why would we not have some guidelines for fighting with the one who is to be closer to us than any other chosen relationship?

> Husbands and wives can prevent a lot of heartache and damage to the marriage if they learn to fight differently.

Many couples have never sat down and drafted their own rules for fighting. I know the idea was completely foreign to my wife and me twenty years ago when we sat down for premarital counseling. Our perspective at the time was simply that people who love each other would just not fight.

Perhaps we had seen that modeled growing up, possibly we had been taught that in church, or maybe we just hoped for the happily ever after without dealing with reality. Bob Goff brought a healthy dose of reality in his book *Love Does* when he wrote, "Jesus talked a lot about disputes, and I'm surprised he never said not to have them... Jesus also talked about how to resolve disputes. He had been the center of quite a few of them, so he would know.[2]"

Patrick Lencioni wrote in *The Five Dysfunctions of a Team*, "It's the lack of conflict that's a problem. Harmony itself is good, if it comes as a result of working through issues constantly and cycling through conflict. But if it comes only as a result of people holding back their opinions and honest concerns, then it's a bad thing.[3]" The fear of conflict produces false harmony, but as the pastor who performed our wedding and walked us through our premarital counseling showed Jennifer and me, conflict without safe guidelines destroys marriages.

Treaty Negotiations

Creating your own rules for fighting is a process that should be carefully and thoughtfully walked through over time. The rules for fighting that our premarital counselor and his wife came up with are not the same that my wife and I have adopted. There may be some similarities and some rules that all couples should include (e.g., hitting your spouse is not acceptable), but there are going to be many variations that will uniquely fit each couple.

> The fear of conflict produces false harmony, but…conflict without safe guidelines destroys marriages.

Here are a few rules for fighting that other couples have adopted that might serve as a good place for you and your spouse to start:

- Assume the best of your spouse.
- Never use never; always avoid using always.
- Be willing to forgive (Matthew 6:15) and accept forgiveness.
- Ten-Minute Rule: Protect the first and last ten minutes of each interaction throughout the day.
- Establish ground rules for taking a break; for example:
  - How do you call for a time out?
  - How long may a time out last (e.g., 20 minutes, 2 hours, 24 hours)?

- o How far can you go on a time out (e.g., can you leave the house?)
  - o Whoever calls for the time out is responsible to re-engage.
- Use "I" statements.
- Don't bring up the past.
- Say what you mean, and mean what you say.
- Don't fight in front of the kids.
- Agree upon a time and place to have argument.
- No yelling, screaming, or profanity.
- Fight the fight you're fighting.
- Agree upon a few selected friends that you can each confide in.
- Avoid turning to family to vent about your spouse's negative qualities.
- Take turns speaking, and avoid speaking over each other.
- Avoid heavy discussions right before bedtime.
- Do not use sex as a weapon.
- Speak of your spouse in public (including social media) as you would want them to speak of you (Luke 6:31).
- Rules are to be self-imposed and not policed by the other spouse (including this rule).

Please do not cut and paste this list and try to apply it to your marriage overnight. The first of the four treaties that make up the Geneva Conventions was written in 1864, with the second in 1906, the third in 1929, and the fourth and final treaty ratified following the Second World War in 1949. What I am getting at is that it takes time and mutual understanding to collaboratively construct a set of guidelines that will serve your marriage in both peace time and times of hostility.

I encourage couples to take their time with this process and begin by drafting the first of many tentative ground rules for fighting. Revisit and revise the tentative list after subsequent times of disagreement until you feel that you may have a set of rules for fighting that truly protects the best interests of the marriage itself. President Richard M. Nixon once said, "We cannot learn from one another until we stop shouting at one another—until we speak quietly enough so that our words can be heard as well as our voices.[4]" Ground rules for fighting help you and your spouse learn better from one another and grow stronger as a couple.

> Ground rules for fighting help you and your spouse learn better from one another and grow stronger as a couple.

The first rule on the preceding list is one that you can begin to apply in advance of treaty negotiations, and that is to assume the best of your spouse. Is he late? Maybe he is helping change a tire for a stranded motorist. Is she not answering your phone calls? Perhaps she is preparing you a surprise dinner. Granted, he may be late because he is inconsiderate, and she may be not answering your calls because she is avoiding you, but let us look at the impact of these two different perspectives.

If you assume the worst or come from a suspicious or pessimistic perspective, you have already negatively impacted the relationship. When we do not truly know what our spouse has done or why they have done what we think that they have done, we do our spouse, ourselves, and our marriage a disservice by not beginning with assuming the best. Recall the shower and hot water example at the end of chapter six: You may not know why your spouse has waited so long to take a shower or has used the last of the hot water; he or she may have done it out of love.

The Apostle Paul said that "[love] does not dishonor others, it is not self-seeking, it is not easily angered, it keeps no record of wrongs. [6]Love does not delight in evil but rejoices with the truth. [7]It always protects, always trusts, always hopes, always perseveres" (I Corinthians 13:5-7, NIV). Love hopes for the best and assumes the best. The truth will come out, and husbands and wives need to address realities in their relationship.

Beginning by assuming the worst or something negative will be picked up by your spouse and may put them on the defensive, which could then trigger a negative cycle. In a sense, you may create a self-fulfilling prophecy by your negative assumption. Why not use your powers for good and not evil and believe in your spouse?

> Why not use your powers for good and not evil and believe in your spouse?

Protect this Spouse

There have been entire books written on forgiveness, and if forgiveness is something that you or your spouse struggles with, it may be in your best interest to pick one up and read it after you finish this book. You may have already heard what C.S. Lewis wrote about forgiveness: "Every one says forgiveness is a lovely idea until they have something to forgive.[5]" Forgiveness can be tough. If it helps, remember that forgiveness is far more about you than about your trespasser.

Forgiveness is largely about making yourself right before God—C.S. Lewis also said, "To be a Christian means to forgive the inexcusable because God has forgiven the inexcusable in you.[6]"—and to free yourself from the never-ending damage that you do to yourself when you harbor unforgiveness. Please do not wait until your spouse has earned the right to be forgiven, or until he or she has shown remorse; neither of those were conditions that Christ gave us prior to Him forgiving us.

Years ago, a couple suggested that they protect the last ten minutes before they leave for work and the first ten minutes after they get home from work and create an argument-free zone. For those two sets of ten minutes, they may not complain, argue, or say anything negative. They determined to protect their marriage and work

> **Forgiveness is largely about making yourself right before God**

at giving their spouse a pleasant memory to carry them through the day as well as to give them something positive to look forward to. After all, who wants to come home to a nagging spouse who complains about the day? When my wife teaches on the ten-minute rule, I often hear her share that these positive ten minutes can erase or undo many of the stresses from the day, and she may even forget about what it was that she had thought to complain about.

Many couples we have worked with have extended this to include the first and last ten minutes of each interaction throughout the day. If one of them needs to complain about something, he or she had better make sure there are twenty-one minutes or more for that phone call. Think about the difference you could make if your spouse knew that each time the two of you were going to see each other after being apart, you were not going to vent, whine, or attack, but instead you were going to greet him or her with joy and leave him or her with positive memories. Following the ten-minute rule will have a positive impact on your perspectives—how you and your spouse see each other—and on your perceptions of each other, thereby creating a more positive reality for your marriage.

We end up with the marriage that we work for. When we begin to evaluate our decisions and actions by asking the question, "How would this make my spouse feel?" and "How does this impact the health of our relationship?" some of our behaviors may need to be changed. Over the years, my wife has mentioned several times that she often does not enjoy hanging out with married women because all too often they sit around and talk negatively about their husbands.

> We end up with the marriage that we work for.

I realize what a blessed man I am to have married a woman who in her very DNA is repulsed by people speaking negatively about their spouse and who chooses to not participate in those conversations. Sure, you may momentarily feel better by venting about your spouse's shortcomings, but each of those statements damages the health of your marriage. The words you speak may eventually come back to your spouse (especially when posted online), and wouldn't you rather them find out that you have been speaking positively about them behind their backs?

So who do you go to when you need to talk to someone about your spouse? The advice that my wife and I received when we were engaged was to mutually agree upon trusted friends that we have permission to go to. These are friends who are not there to take sides but who can provide a listening ear and godly counsel.

If you are unable to identity friends who have healthy marriages you respect and might serve as these trusted confidants, enlist the help of a licensed Christian counselor in your area. Who knows, you may find yourself sitting on a couch with three cushions, and you will already know why.

Eighteen

White Socks

You thought you had white socks until Christmas. There are some things in life that we believe because they are true, but as this book has tried to help you see, there are also some things in life that we believe because our perceptions are greater than reality. When we are able to see from a new perspective, our perceptions are challenged, and we have an opportunity to understand more accurately. You, like so many other people, thought that you had white socks until Christmas.

There were a few things that I could count on receiving each Christmas: a new tooth brush, some Christmas candy, some piece of fruit that would go right back into the refrigerator, and a pack of white socks. After assembling a new set of Lego bricks, I would eventually have to bring my new Christmas clothes upstairs and put them away in my bedroom. The shirts would go in the middle drawer, my new jeans in the bottom drawer, and my new white socks in the top drawer.

Freshly folded out of the package and still with an odd piece of clear tape on them that helped them keep their shape, the new white socks were a noticeably different color than all of the other socks that took up residence in the sock drawer, revealing a truth I had not previously seen. The simple truth is that I thought I had white socks until I saw what a pair of white socks looked like. The new white socks helped to challenge my perceptions of what I had, and I was invited to accept a new reality of what a white sock is.

How is your marriage? Are you and your spouse good at communicating? Do you truly know and understand your spouse? I have worked with countless couples who have felt that they were fine and took for granted that their marriage was a pair of white socks until they had the Christmas-morning experience of seeing what a pair of white socks could look like. This book is for you and your marriage and not just for your spouse or someone else's marriage. This book is an invitation for you to be ambitiously curious about your spouse and how you can better your relationship.

The White Socks Test

I realize what I am asking of some of you who have gotten this far and still do not see any pressing need to challenge your perceptions. I cannot recall ever celebrating a single Thanksgiving when I was concerned with whether or not my socks were truly white. Let us be honest, who cares how white a pair of socks is? The health and strength of our marriage is a completely different question and one that often literally has eternal consequences. So how do you do the white socks test for your marriage? Here are a few suggestions that my wife and I often offer:

- Ask better questions.
- Don't trust your gut.
- Study your spouse.
- Explore the exchange rate for foreign deposits into your love banks.
- Seek to regularly learn something new about your spouse.
- Learn your Love Languages.
- Learn your spouse's Love Languages.

- Seek to understand before being understood.
- When you find yourself getting upset, let it be a red flag that something else is going on.
- The goal is not to change your spouse, but to change how you see them.

The goal here is to truly find out how well you know your spouse and to better understand the areas that need growth in your marriage. One of the best ways to obtain some objective information about your relationship is to sit down with a counselor who is trained to administer a marriage assessment tool like Life Innovation's ENRICH[1], but you would be amazed at how much you can learn about your spouse and relationship just by asking better questions.

Questions, by their very nature, are intended to uncover new information, and I have found that some spouses are just better at asking questions than others. "How was your day?" followed by the perfunctory response "Fine" does not truly communicate much useable information. "Honey, tell me how your day was today" may go a long way in helping you get a better feel for what your spouse's day was like.

There is still a good chance that you will receive "Fine" as the response, but you can follow up with an even better question: "What was fine about it?", "What made it a fine day?", "How so?", or my personal favorite for use in a session, "What does fine look like to you?"

You have got to want to know how your spouse's day was and convey that message. If you do not care, or if your spouse perceives you do not care, he or she is not likely going to waste the time and energy to

You have got to want to know how your spouse's day was and convey that message.

verbally relive the day for you.

All too often on a Sunday morning, people will ask me how I am doing as they continue their stroll to the sanctuary or in the other direction to pick up their kids from the children's ministry center. They do not appear interested, nor do they look as if they have the time, to hear how I am really doing, and they may hear me respond with one of the socially acceptable replies of good, great, fine, or fantastic. May we not have socially acceptable canned responses for our spouse.

Study Thy Spouse

One of the benefits of being in a long-term relationship is that you get to know each other well and you feel you know each other well enough to know what the other is thinking and to be able to finish each other's sentences. One of the drawbacks of being in a long-term relationship is that you are often wrong. You may think you knew what your spouse was thinking, but you were wrong. The best way to know is to ask. I often invite couples who are struggling with communication to simply not trust their gut for a while.

> I often invite couples who are struggling with communication to simply not trust their gut for a while.

If you think you know what the other is thinking, stop and ask. Do not assume that your instincts are accurate. Do not trust your gut, but verify so that you can acquire a new set of accurate data points from which to build better future assumptions. No matter how well you felt you knew your spouse, he or she likely changed since then. As the ancient Greek philosopher Heraclitus said, "You can never step into the same river; for new waters are always flowing on you," reminding us that people grow, mature, and change over time.

I guarantee you that there is something you do not know about your spouse. You could learn something new about your spouse each and every day until the Lord calls you home, and there would still be more to learn. Study your spouse. Day 18 of *The Love Dare* reads, "Consider the following perspective: if the amount you studied your spouse before marriage were equal to a high school diploma, then you should continue to learn about your mate until you gain a 'college degree,' a 'master's degree,' and ultimately a 'doctorate degree'.[2]" Become a lifelong learner of your spouse, and it will pay dividends to your relationship.

Part of becoming a lifelong learner may also include learning the exchange rate of foreign deposits made into each other's love bank. My wife and I grew up in northeastern Massachusetts. We were less than a four-hour car ride from the Canadian border. Canadian quarters look an awful lot like U.S. quarters, and it was common practice for stores to accept Canadian coins. Chances are they would then give out those Canadian coins to the next customer requiring change. When we moved to southeastern Pennsylvania for Bible College, we learned rather quickly that Canadian coins held no value there. I mean, literally zero. There was no exchange rate at Bob's Haven Deli; a Canadian Quarter was worthless there, despite holding real

> Part of becoming a lifelong learner may also include learning the exchange rate of foreign deposits made into each other's love bank.

monetary value just 450 miles to the north.

In thriving relationships, husbands and wives have learned the actions and words that have intrinsic value to their spouse and know the exchange rate for foreign deposits. I can hold the door open for my wife when we go on a date, and although she is quite capable of holding the door open for herself, she is able to deposit my gesture as an act of love into her love bank. There are a lot of foods that I do not like to eat, and I mean a lot of foods, but during the early years of our marriage, I was able to receive meals my wife cooked as deposits into my love bank even though I never deposited any of the food into my stomach.

Those of you reading this book who have children may be able to appreciate when your child has made you a gift and you instinctively exchange their homemade expression of love and receive it as a deposit into your love bank. The better you are able to appreciate your spouse organizing your golf clubs, scheduling your colonoscopy, or inviting your parents over for dinner as foreign currency deposits into your love bank, the healthier your account balances will be. We also need to learn the exchange rate for our intentional efforts to make deposits into their love banks. We may not receive full-face value for our foreign currency—growing up we used the estimate of one U.S. dollar to $1.25 Canadian currency—but there is no sense in dismissing good deposits as without worth.

> Your spouse is not the enemy, but your lack of truly knowing the one you are married to will lead to battle scars.

The Art of Marriage

The goal here is to better understand your spouse so that

you can more effectively communicate your love for them to them. Sun Tzu wrote in *The Art of War*, "If you know your enemies and know yourself, you will not be imperiled in a hundred battles... if you do not know your enemies nor yourself, you will be imperiled in every single battle.[3]" Your spouse is not the enemy, but the same underlying principle remains true. Let me repeat that for clarity: Your spouse is not the enemy, but your lack of truly knowing the one you are married to will lead to battle scars. Falsely assuming that you know your spouse more than you actually do will also lead to battle scars, and you will be blindsided by the damage.

Taking a step back and consciously choosing to not trust your gut but endeavoring to study your spouse can be one of the best decisions that you can make to improve your relationship. In his book *Explorations in Marital and Family Therapy*, James Framo wrote, "People do not marry people, not real ones anyway; they marry what they think the person is; they marry illusions and images. The exciting adventure of marriage is finding out who the partner really is.[4]"

Imagine with me the following scenario. Husband comes home after a day in the office, and after taking off his coat, he rolls up his sleeves and walks into the kitchen to prepare dinner. His wife is in the living room sitting on the couch. While cooking dinner, he decides to wash the dishes that remained in the sink and then sets the table for dinner. Dinner is going to take some time to finish cooking, so he decides he might as well start a load of laundry.

Husband notices a load in the dryer and proceeds to fold laundry and deliver the freshly cleaned clothes to each bedroom in the house. By now, dinner is ready, and he brings all of the prepared food to the dining room table and invites his wife to join him. Husband is rather excited because he is certain that he has just won "man of the year" and begins to think through which head shot he would submit for the cover photo of *Time Magazine.*

Wife, however, is wondering if her husband even loves her anymore, begins to suspect that he is having an affair, and starts to cry. She had been sitting in the living room on the couch, eagerly gazing out the window like a love-crazed teenager, counting the moments until her true love returned from work. She is rather tired from her busy day, but she springs off the couch with anticipation when she sees his car turn into their driveway; that was the last happy feeling she remembers from that evening.

When husband came inside, he said hello, but then proceeded to ignore her and walked straight into the kitchen. He did not hug her, kiss her, or stop to give her five minutes of his time before getting lost in a never-ending list of chores he must view as more important than his wife. Wife fumed, she sulked, she cried, and she fumed again, before she was finally acknowledged again by her husband after what seemed like an eternity later, when he invited her to join him at the table for dinner.

What Language Do You Speak?

What is going on here with our husband and wife? Well, if you have read Gary Chapman's book *The Five Love Languages*[5] (and I highly recommend that you do), you may recognize that husband and wife are each speaking very different languages. In *The Five Love Languages,* the author suggests that there are several different types of ways that we show and receive love, and he calls these tendencies love languages. The language that you use to receive love tends to be the language you also understand for giving love. If you are not "fluent" in one or more of the five love languages, then you may not understand or interpret the actions spoken via that language as an act of love. The five love languages discussed in Gary Chapman's books are:

- Words of Affirmation
- Acts of Service
- Receiving Gifts
- Quality Time
- Physical Touch

Clearly, husband fluently speaks Acts of Service, and from the vignette, I suspect that wife speaks Quality Time and/or Physical Touch. Husband and wife no doubt need to work on their communication skills, but they also need to understand what their own love languages are and what their spouse's love languages are. You may feel that your husband does not want to spend time with you, but lay his actions down and compare them to what those acts of service mean to him, and you may arrive at a different conclusion. You may also believe that you are doing an outstanding job communicating to your spouse how much you love him or her, but if you compare your perceptions to your spouse's perceptions, you may find that perceived realities are not matching up.

> [I]f you compare your perceptions to your spouse's perceptions, you may find that perceived realities are not matching up.

Do not just continue being confident that your socks are white; see how they stack up. Some individuals spend too much time and energy trying to get others, including their spouse, to understand their point of view and not enough energy trying to understand the point of view of others. Seek to understand before being understood.

When you see your spouse getting upset, interpret that response as a red flag that something else is going on. Sure, you were late and they chose to get mad, but more importantly, what does it mean to them that you were late?

When you find yourself feeling your emotions rise during conflict, be able to take a step back and ask yourself some tough questions, seeking to get to the root of why you are responding the way you are responding.

Spending time with quality friends who have healthy marriages, attending weekend marriage conferences, reading good books on marriage, seeking marriage counseling, and being a part of a small group focused on building thriving marriages are just a few more tangible ways that you can do the white socks test on a routine basis. My parents rarely bought me new white socks throughout the year, but you do not need to wait until next Christmas to take a good honest look at the strength and quality of your marriage.

> Do not just continue being confident that your socks are white; see how they stack up.

I know the laundry detergent industry spends millions of dollars trying to convince you that you and your children have to have the whitest socks to be a happy family, but who really cares about how white they are? The health of your marriage is a completely different issue altogether, and there are no international corporations spending millions of dollars promoting healthy, sparkling marriages. Your marriage needs you to become its best advocate and intentionally find ways to make it sparkle.

Nineteen

Hello, My Name Is: Reality

A young couple moves into a new neighborhood. The next morning while they are eating breakfast, the young woman sees her neighbor hanging the wash outside. "That laundry is not very clean; she doesn't know how to wash correctly. Perhaps she needs better laundry soap." Her husband looks on, remaining silent. Every time her neighbor hangs her wash to dry, the young woman makes the same comments. A month later, the woman is surprised to see clean laundry on the line and says to her husband, "Look, she has learned how to wash correctly. I wonder who taught her this." The husband says, "I got up early this morning and cleaned our windows."

You have probably read that story online or heard it used as a sermon illustration before; it reminds us of how much our perception of reality is influenced by what we see. This short illustration also highlights the influence your heart and your character have on the reality that your perceptions, and perspective, help to create. C.S. Lewis perhaps said it best: "For what you see and hear depends a good deal on where you are standing: it also depends on what sort of person you are.[1]"

There is so much in life that truly is not what you think it is, what you believe it is, or even how it looks to you. There are so many different forces that influence what you think you see, and you will make life-altering decisions and choices based upon your perceptions. The Bible reminds us that "the heart is deceitful above all things" (Jeremiah 17:9a), and if we are truthful with ourselves, we realize that we bear more of the responsibility for the current state of the health of our marriage than we may have been willing to admit when we first picked up this book.

My personal prayer for you and for your marriage is that there have been some practical tools within these chapters to help you get your marriage where it needs to be to thrive. Perhaps more important, I have prayed that this book itself would be a tool to help you see your marriage like never before. Hello, my name is reality, and I can be one of the best friends your marriage has ever known.

You are about to complete reading this book, and it is my prayer that you will walk away with a clearer perspective and more accurate perceptions, but this book is just the beginning and has only scratched the surface. Some of the perceptions you have held have been the only reality you have known for so long that it may take time, a process, to uncover new truths layer

> There is so much in life that truly is not what you think it is, what you believe it is, or even how it looks to you.

by layer. Having now read some of the practical tips, tools, and techniques in these later chapters, you may benefit from reading the first half of this book over again. Then, having re-read the earlier chapters, you may benefit from re-reading these later chapters.

I guess I am suggesting that you read the book twice so that you can have read both the theoretical and the practical before reading the practical and theoretical. Maybe you are not in a place right now where you feel that you can go back and re-read the entire book, so if there is one thing to take away from this book, it would be this: **Your perspectives inform your perceptions, and your perceptions are greater than reality**.

Flat Earth Society

There is a good reason so many quality books, conferences, retreats, and, yes, even sermons fall short of transforming your marriage from what it is to what you desire it to be. They can fail to bring about the needed change because you have been stuck with the same incomplete perspectives and false perceptions that were problematic to begin with. If you believe the world is flat, then you will dismiss or fail to understand any teachings on GPS navigation, satellite TV, and the moon orbiting the earth as the earth orbits the sun because they all require a round earth.

The fact that you may believe the earth is flat, and it may even appear flat for your point of view, prevents you from accepting or grasping truths that are built upon the premise that the earth is not flat[2]. Your belief that the world is flat does not change the truth about satellites being able to orbit the earth—helping us navigate the city streets, tune in and watch a live sports broadcast, or predict the cycles of the moon or seasons—but your belief that the world is flat prevents you from believing that any of these scientific advancements were possible.

> A husband is simply not going to try to listen better to his wife's concerns if he believes that her concerns are irrational and invalid.

A husband is simply not going to try to listen better to his wife's concerns if he believes that her concerns are irrational and invalid. A new perspective and subsequent perceptions of the value of his wife's concerns are required in order for him to see the value in what she has to say.

You can listen to the greatest sermon ever preached on Ephesians 5:25 (Husbands, love your wives, just as Christ loved the church and gave himself up for her), but without a willingness to change your perspective or challenge your perceptions, you will remain as lost and misinformed as the prisoners chained in Plato's allegorical cave.

> **I do not want you to be lost or a prisoner, and neither does God.**

I do not want you to be lost or a prisoner, and neither does God. I believe that is why He has brought us together through the pages of this book.

You Are the Man

In perhaps my favorite perspective/perception example in Scripture, God chose to use the prophet Nathan. In 2 Samuel chapter 12 God sends the prophet Nathan to confront David following his sins recorded in chapter 11. Nathan tells King David a story:

> There were two men in a certain town, one rich and the other poor. 2 The rich man had a very large number of sheep and cattle, 3but the poor man had nothing except one little ewe lamb he had bought. He raised it, and it grew up with him and his children. It shared his food, drank from his cup and even slept in his arms. It was like a daughter to him. 4 Now a traveler came to the rich man, but the rich man refrained from taking one of his own sheep or cattle to prepare a meal for the traveler who had come to him. Instead, he took the ewe lamb that belonged to the poor man and prepared it for the

one who had come to him. (2 Samuel 12:1b-4, NIV)

Nathan could have directly confronted David with his sin, but instead he relies upon the wisdom of God, who knew David's heart. David views the world through the eyes of a divinely appointed king (his perspective), and he believes that he can do whatever he pleases and have what or whoever he desires (his perception). As such, his response to Nathan reveals that he clearly has no understanding that the story is about him… yet. King David needs to be re-acclimated to the truth and to be reintroduced to real reality, but first, Nathan allows David to condemn himself by his own words:

> [5] David burned with anger against the man and said to Nathan, "As surely as the Lord lives, the man who did this must die! [6] He must pay for that lamb four times over, because he did such a thing and had no pity." (2 Samuel 12:5-6, NIV)

The contrast between 2 Samuel chapter 11 and chapter 12 reveals the two sides to David's heart. Here in chapter 12, he recognizes right from wrong, but time and time again in chapter 11, David's perceptions obfuscate the truth. God uses the prophet Nathan to clarify truth from fiction and re-acclimate David to reality with four simple words: "You are the man!" Nathan then goes on to tell David that he has done wrong by arranging for Uriah's death and taking Uriah's wife as his own, how it has grieved God, and what the consequences for his actions will be.

David's perspective was accurate yet incomplete and therefore wrong.

David's narrow perspective focused his sight on his authority as king and what he could do. Just like the blind men with the elephant in the Indian parable, David's perspective was accurate yet incomplete and therefore wrong. All of us, like David, have a choice to make when confronted with the truth. When David was confronted with God's perspective, he saw his actions for what they were, and Scripture records, "[13]Then David said to Nathan, 'I have sinned against the Lord'." (2 Samuel 12:13a, NIV) Verse 13 records that God accepted David's contrite heart, and He not only forgave him of his sins, but He also spared his life.

There is power in correcting or completing inaccurate or incomplete perspectives. David's change in perspective saved his life. Sadly, David's perceptions and the lies that he had accepted as reality cost him the life of his son. I do not know what decisions you have made in your life because of your previously held perspectives and perceptions, nor do I know the prices you may have paid. I do know that God has better things in store for your tomorrows and that you can start living them today. We just have to be willing to accept God's Truth, repent, and ask for forgiveness when He shows us the errors of our ways.

Now, you may have never sent a man to the front lines of battle, and you may have never had an adulterous affair that produced a child, but if Romans 3:23 ("For all have sinned…") is to be believed, then we all have some growing edges that God would like to spend some time talking to us about. I invite you to ask God what some of those might be in your life before you get to the end of this book. If you are reading this book now for the second time, as long as Romans 3:23 remains true, then this still applies to you. As God challenges your perceptions and asks you to alter your reality, may I encourage you with the strongest words possible to have a heart more like King David and less like King Saul (see 1 Samuel 15).

Risky Business

The most common misperception I come across when talking with husbands and wives is that "we are fine," or, perhaps more accurate, "we are good enough." These couples have not checked how white their socks are, they have not turned on the lights to see the whole elephant, and they are not aiming for the moon. In their defense, they are getting by, but at what cost and what sacrifice? I suspect if you have come this far, then you are striving to beat the statistics and fight for God's best for your marriage.

> [O]ur tolerance to accept risk when we have the perception of having some control over the outcome empowers us to take risks for ourselves that we might deem foolish for others.

We have some forces that tend to work against us, though, and one of them is our tolerance to accept risk. More specifically, our tolerance to accept risk when we have the perception of having some control over the outcome empowers us to take risks for ourselves that we might deem foolish for others.

In 1969, Chauncey Stars conducted a study on risk perception and discovered that people were willing to accept risks that were 1,000 times greater if they perceived they were in control of the risk than if they did not[3]. The classic example of risks we are willing to accept is driving a car versus a nuclear disaster. The reality is, far too many of us accept risks everyday with our marriages that defy logic. Our decisions to accept risks are also influenced by survivorship bias, as we focus on what we can see and inadvertently overlook what has not survived.

Survivorship Bias

Army Air Force bombers were being shot down at an alarming rate during World War II. After the surviving planes were analyzed, the decision was made to reinforce the areas that showed the most damage from enemy attacks, but this did not provide any needed help. The death rate held steady until mathematician Abraham Wald suggested reinforcing the parts of the planes that were returning from flight without showing any damage[4,5]. Why? The areas of the planes that showed the most enemy damage were the wings, body, and tail gunners, so Wald accurately concluded that these areas were able to receive damage and still be survivable. The areas of the plane that, when damaged, were not survivable were not observed because those planes did not survive and did not return from combat flights.

> [F]ar too many of us accept **risks** everyday with our marriages that **defy** logic.

What am I getting at here? In life, we as individuals may metaphorically bolster the armor on our jobs, financial security, or reputation because these are the things that we see as "under attack." But our inaccurate perceptions of what is most vulnerable can put us at great risk and lead us to not protect the very things that are the most important to the survival of our marriage.

We may even be willing to take extraordinary risks with our marriage because we perceive that we are in control of the risk. Protect your marriage. You may have no idea how much your inattention to detail may impact the health and stability of your relationship. Each day, each decision, each opportunity matters.

Andy Stanley wrote, "The measure of a man [sic] or woman's character is not determined by a fill-in-the-blank or true-or-false exam. This is an essay test. An essay that takes a lifetime to write. Today you wrote a section.[6]" Think of your marriage in a similar manner because your marriage takes a lifetime to write. Today you are writing another section. You may not see the results immediately, but one day you will, for better or for worse.

> **Protect** your marriage. You may have no idea how much your inattention to detail may impact the **health** and **stability** of your relationship.

God also intended marriage to be until death do us part, so pace yourself for the life-long journey. Remember, God does not look at things the same way that you and I do (see 1 Samuel 16:7), and the more like Jesus we are and the more we accept God's perspective, the better off we will be. When your brief time here on earth is coming to a close, how will you define a life successfully lived?

The Game of Life

Our family received the board game The Game of Life as a gift a few years ago. We were playing as a family, with my wife Jennifer and our then six-year-old daughter, Hailey, on one team, our eight-year-old daughter, Autumn, and I on the second team, and our four-year-old son, Christian, with his own car to drive around the board. Jennifer and Hailey's team won, and after the game was over, I overheard Hailey softly consoling Autumn by saying, "Sorry you didn't win." To this, Autumn replied that she was the banker and ended the game with the most money! Earlier, during the game, I had commented that the bank loses the most money—Jennifer and I had received over 2.5 million dollars—and that the banker had lost more money than anyone else. It truly all does come down to perspective. Christian also kept claiming that he had won because he drove all the way to the end with light sabers (the boy and girl pegs)!

You and I may be free to make up our own rules when playing a board game, but when it comes to life, God alone has that role. You and I can argue all we want, we can pretend all we want, and we can even try to ignore truth and reality all we want. In the end, our perspectives and perceptions do not make something true, no matter how strongly we believe it to be true.

> In the end, our perspectives and perceptions **do not make something true**, no matter how **strongly** we **believe** it to be true.

As has been said before, the main difference between human beings and God is that God never thinks He is us. When we humbly approach God and allow Him full control over our hopes, dreams, desires, marriage, and life, we find a life that is truly worth living.

Living with the one we love, growing old together, and sharing our lives with each other are great gifts that God gives us as husbands and wives. Marriage is a lot of work; building a thriving marriage is even more work. I do not know what the current state of your marriage is, but I do know that God has even bigger and greater things for you and your spouse.

If you are willing to invest some blood, sweat, tears, and time productively, then God will do some amazing things. If you are willing to look at your marriage from a different perspective, and if you are open to challenging some of your perceptions, then a whole new reality is waiting for you, a reality that Martin Luther described as "Let the wife make her husband glad to come home, and let him make her sorry to see him leave." So pull up a chair, or better yet, grab one of the three cushions on the couch, aim for the moon, and see what God has in store for your marriage.

ENDNOTES

Chapter 1

1. Yancey, P. (2000). *Reaching for the invisible God.* Grand Rapids, MI: Zondervan.
2. Collins, J. (2001). *Good to great: Why some companies make the leap…and others don't.* New York, NY: Collins.

Chapter 2

1. The Potomac Ministry Network created an event the call *NEXT: Leading a generation to take the next step* that is organized by John May and hosted by Mark Batterson. Dick Foth is a longtime friend of both the Potomac Ministry Network and Mark Batterson and during the spring of 2012 he was one of the invited guest speakers.
2. Merton, T. (1955). *No man is an island.* New York, NY: Harcourt Brace.
3. Robert J. Wicks is professor emeritus at Loyola University Maryland in the Pastoral Counseling Department. He has authored nearly two dozen books and while teaching at Loyola was well-known for his seminar-like Pastoral Integration course (PC700.51). This quote was from the morning of February 9, 2006, but neither the first nor last time that he had shared it with students.
4. Smalley, G. (2004). *The DNA of relationships.* Wheaton, IL: Tyndale.
5. Lewis, C. S. (1955). *Surprised by joy.* San Diego, CA: Harcourt Brace.

Chapter 3

1. For more information on Motivational Interviewing see Miller, W. R. & Rollnick, S. (2012). *Motivational interviewing: Helping people change* (3rd ed.). New York, NY: Guildford Press.
2. Attributed to George Bernard Shaw (1856-1950).
3. Attributed to Henry Ford (1863-1947).

Chapter 4

1. The story of the blind men and an elephant has its origins in the Indian subcontinent, but has since spread around the globe and across religions. Variations include the men being blind or in the dark; the number of men around the elephant (most often five or six); and whether the men come to the resolution on their own in the dark or when it becomes light (for those not blind), or by the addition of another man who sees the entire elephant or is an omniscient narrator. One of the most notable versions may be American poet John Godfey Saxe's poem (1872) "The Blind Men and the Elephant" that was later sung by Natalie Merchant (2010). The story has been used to promote peace, war, physics, biology, various religious faith traditions and even told from the perspective of the elephant who jokes that "men are flat".
2. Emerson, R. W. (1982). *Emerson in his journals*. J. Porte (Ed.). Cambridge, MA: Harvard University Press.

Chapter 5

1. City of Refuge Network (cityofrefugenetwork.org) was founded in 2010 by Brian Griswold and Dr. Jason Karampatsos as a counseling ministry to pastors, missionaries, evangelists, and their spouses and families seeking professional Christian counseling from someone who understands the unique pressures of serving in ministry. Both co-founders are ordained ministers and licensed clinical professional counselors with extensive backgrounds and training in working with both the psychological and spiritual and provide preventative, supportive, and restorative counseling to individuals, couples, and families.

2. Focus on the Family, as part of their *The Pastor's Advocate Series: Ministering to the needs of your minister*, reported in *Living in the Pastor's Home* (2012) by Marshall Shelley and Bob Moeller (Dan Davidson, Ed.) excerpts from London, H. B. (1992). The home litmus test. *Leadership*. 13(4), 14-23.

3. Kurtz, G. (Producer), & Lucas, G. (Director). (1977). Star wars episode IV: A new hope. (Motion picture). United States. 20th Century Fox.

4. Attributed to Albert Einstein (1879-1955).

5. Lincoln, A. (1965). *Abraham Lincoln: Wisdom and wit*. L. Bachelder (Ed.). Mount Vernon, NY: Pauper Press.

Chapter 6

1. Covey, S. (1989). *The 7 habits of highly effective people: Powerful lessons in personal change*. New York, NY: Simon & Schuster.

2. The "7 billion people on this planet" statement is based on the United States Census Bureau (census.gov) estimate that the world surpassed 7 billion people on March 12, 2012 and United

Nations Population Fund (unfpa.org) estimate that the world surpassed 7 billion on October 31, 201.
3. Tolstoy, L. (1962). *Fables & fairy tales*. New York, NY: Signet Classics.
4. Thoreau H. D. (1993). A year in Thoreau's journal, 1851. New York, NY: Penguin. Books.

Chapter 7

1. The original complete quote is, *"prima societas in ipso conjugio est; proxima in liberis; deinde una domus, communia omnia"* which translates as, "The first bond of society is marriage; the next, our children; then the whole family and all things in common". Marcus Tullius Cicero (106 BC – 43 BC): Influential Roman philosopher, politician, lawyer, and public speaker.
2. Bromley, D. G. (1997). 1994 Presidential address remembering the future: A sociological narrative of crisis episodes, collective action, culture workers, and counter movements. *Sociology of Religion, 58*, 105-140. Available from http://socrel.oxfordjournals.org
3. Ripley, J. S., Worthington, E. L., Jr., Bromley, D., & Kemper, S. D. (2005). Covenantal and contractual values in marriage: Marital values orientation toward wedlock or self-actualization (marital VOWS) scale. *Personal Relationships, 12*, 317-336. doi:10.1111/j.1475-6811.2005.00118.x
4. Olson, D. H., & DeFrain, J. (1997). Marriage and the family: Diversity and strengths.(2nd Ed.) Mountain View, CA: Mayfield Publishing.
5. Kreider, R. M., & Ellis, R. (2011). Number, timing and duration of marriages and divorces: 2009. *Current Population Reports* (Census Bureau Publication P70-125). Washington, DC: U.S.

Census Bureau. Retrieved from
http://www.census.gov/prod/2011pubs/p70-125.pdf

6. Pew Research Center Social and Demographic
Trends (2010). The decline of marriage and rise of
new families. *Pew Research Center.* Retrieved
from www.pewsocialtrends.org/ 2010/11/18/the-
decline-of-marriage-and-rise-of-new-families/

7. Barna, G. (1993). *The future of the American
family.* Chicago: Moody Press.

8. Barna Group (2008). New marriage and divorce
statistics released. Retrieved from
www.barna.org/barna-update/article/15-
familykids/42-new-marriage-and-divorce-statistics-
released

9. Tejada-Vera, B., & Sutton, P. D. (2010) Births,
marriages, divorces, and deaths: Provisional data for
2009. *National Vital Statistics Reports, 58(25) 1-6.*
Retrieved from http://www.cdc.gov

10. Kreider, R. M., & Fields, J. M. (2001). Number,
timing and duration of marriages and divorces: Fall
1996. *Current Population Reports* (Census Bureau
Publication No. P70-80). Washington DC: U.S.
Census Bureau. Retrieved from
www.census.gov/prod/2002pubs/p70-80.pdf

11. Pew Research Center Social and Demographic
Trends (2010). The decline of marriage and rise of
new families. *Pew Research Center.* Retrieved
from www.pewsocialtrends.org/ 2010/11/18/the-
decline-of-marriage-and-rise-of-new-families/

12. Pinsof, W. M. (2002). The death of 'till death us do
part': The transformation of pair-bonding in the 20th
century. *Family Process, 41*, 135-157.
doi:10.1111/j.1545-5300.2002.41202.x

13. Pew Forum on Religion and Public Life (2008).
U.S. religious landscape survey. *Pew Research*

Center. Retrieved from
religions.pewforum.org/reports

14. Tozer, A. W. (1961). The knowledge of the holy:
The attributes of God, their meaning in the
Christian life. New York, NY. Harper & Row.
15. The accounts of these five men, and what the Bible
records of their wives and marriages, are recorded
in the Old Testament: Job (in the book of Job);
Noah (Genesis chapters 6-9); Abraham (Genesis
chapters 12-25); Jacob (Genesis chapters 25-49);
and Potiphar (Genesis chapter 39).
16. Bromley, D. G. (1997). 1994 Presidential address
remembering the future: A sociological narrative of
crisis episodes, collective action, culture workers,
and counter movements. *Sociology of Religion, 58*,
105-140. Available from socrel.oxfordjournals.org
17. The Abrahamic Covenant found in Genesis chapters
12-17 is known as the *Brit bein HaBetarim* (the
Covenant Between the Parts) in Hebrew. The
Covenant (or three Covenants) promises to make
Abraham a great nation and bless him (Genesis
12:1-3), to give Abraham's descendants all the land
from the river of Egypt to the Euphrates (Genesis
15:18-21), and to make Abraham the father of many
nations and to give his descendant's the whole land
of Canaan (Genesis 17:1-9). Abraham and every
male descendant and loving among them was to be
circumcised (Genesis 17:9-14).
18. The Noahic Covenant is found in Genesis 9
following the flood and the appearance of a rainbow
in the sky. God's covenant with Jacob is found in
Genesis 28:10-22 and referenced in Exodus 2:24,
Leviticus 26:42, and 2 Kings 13:23. The Mosaic
Covenant is recorded in Exodus 19-24 and the Ten
Commandments were given for the Israelites to
uphold as their end of the covenant. The Davidic

Covenant in 2 Samuel 7 established David and his descendants as the kings of the united kingdom of Israel.

19. The Council of Chalcedon (AD 451) is named after the city in Asia Minor where this fourth Ecumenical Council was held with approximately 370 church leaders from the Eastern Orthodox Church, the Roman Catholic Church, the Old Catholics, and various other Western Christian groups. The Council of Chalcedon issued the Chalcedonian Definition which declared the two natures in one person of Jesus Christ:

Following, then, the holy Fathers, we all unanimously teach that our Lord Jesus Christ is to us One and the same Son, the Self-same Perfect in Godhead, the Self-same Perfect in Manhood; truly God and truly Man; the Self-same of a rational soul and body; co-essential with the Father according to the Godhead, the Self-same co-essential with us according to the Manhood; like us in all things, sin apart; before the ages begotten of the Father as to the Godhead, but in the last days, the Self-same, for us and for our salvation (born) of Mary the Virgin Theotokos as to the Manhood; One and the Same Christ, Son, Lord, Only-begotten; acknowledged in Two Natures unconfusedly, unchangeably, indivisibly, inseparably; the difference of the Natures being in no way removed because of the Union, but rather the properties of each Nature being preserved, and (both) concurring into One Person and One Hypostasis; not as though He were parted or divided into Two Persons, but One and the Self-same Son and Only-begotten God, Word, Lord, Jesus Christ; even as from the beginning the prophets have taught concerning Him, and as the

Lord Jesus Christ Himself hath taught us, and as the Symbol of the Fathers hath handed down to us.
20. Quote attributed to Martin Luther (1483-1546), perhaps most known for *The Ninety-Five Theses* that he famously nailed to the door of the All Saints Church in Wittenberg on October 31, 1517 sparking the Reformation.
21. http://2010.census.gov

Chapter 8
1. The United States Census Bureau estimated that there is a birth every 8 seconds and a death every 11 seconds in America with a net gain every 14 seconds increasing the population estimates.
2. Kreider, R. M., & Ellis, R. (2011). Number, timing and duration of marriages and divorces: 2009. *Current Population Reports* (Census Bureau Publication P70-125). Washington, DC: U.S. Census Bureau. Retrieved from http://www.census.gov/prod/2011pubs/p70-125.pdf
3. Lewis, C. S. (1952). *Mere Christianity*. New York, NY. Macmillan.
4. The Biblical account of God parting the Red Sea is found in Exodus 13:17-14:29; providing water from a rock is found in Exodus 17:1-7 ("*strike the rock*") and Numbers 20:1-13 ("speak to the rock"); raising Lazarus from the dead is recorded in John 11:38-44; and all four Gospels give an account of Jesus feeding the 5,000 with 5 loaves and 2 fishes (Matthew 14:31-21; Mark 6:31-44; Luke 9:10-17; John 6:5-15).
5. Solution focused brief therapy (SFBT) is, as its name clearly implies, focused on finding solutions to the problem that brought the client in for counseling in a single session or a brief series of sessions. Social workers Steve de Shazer and Insoo

Kim Berg are credited with developing SFBT and Teri Pichot and Yvonne M Dolan (2003) have co-authoured the text book *Solution-focused brief therapy:Its effective use in agency settings* (New York, NY: Routledge).

In Insoo Kim Berg and Yvonne M Dolan (2001) book *Tales of solutions: A collection of hope-inspiring stories* (New York, NY: W. W. Norton & Company) they share the following example of the Miracle Question as used in a SFBT counseling session. "I am going to ask you a rather strange question (pause). The strange question is this: (pause) After we talk, you will go back to your work (home, school) and you will do whatever you need to do the rest of today, such as taking care of the children, cooking dinner, watching TV, giving the children a bath, and so on. It will be time to go to bed. Everybody in your household is quiet, and you are sleeping in peace. In the middle of the night, a miracle happens and the problem that prompted you to talk to me today is solved! But because this happens while you are sleeping, you have no way of knowing that there was an overnight miracle that solved the problem. (pause) So, when you wake up tomorrow morning, what might be the small change that will make you say to yourself, 'Wow, something must have happened—the problem is gone!'"?

6. The Moon's orbit around the Earth is elliptical, and as such the distance between the Moon and the Earth varies throughout the year. According to NASA, the actual distance varies from between 225,623 miles (perigee) and 252,088 miles (apogee). solarsystem.nasa.gov/planets/profile.cfm?Display=Facts&Object=Moon

7. Eiseley, L. C. (1969). *The unexpected universe.* New York, NY: Harcourt, Brace & World.

8. Although the phrase "One Day at a Time" and the origins of the Serenity Prayer predate Alcoholics Anonymous, "In creating A.A., the Serenity Prayer has been a most valuable building block-indeed a cornerstone." A long version of the prayer is often recited as follows: *God grant me the SERENITY to accept the things I cannot change; COURAGE to change the things I can; and WISDOM to know the difference. Living one day at a time; enjoying one moment at a time; accepting hardships as the pathway to peace; taking, as He did, this sinful world as it is, not as I would have it: Trusting that He will make all things right if I surrender to His Will; that I may be reasonably happy in this life and supremely happy with Him forever in the next. Amen* (source www.aahistory.com/prayer.html)

9. Morris, J. (Producer). Stanton, A. (Director). (2008). *WALL-E.* (Motion picture). United States: Walt Disney Home Entertainment.

Chapter 9

1. If you are like me, you likely would like to see the cartoon that I referenced at the beginning of this chapter. Although the cartoon is unsigned, it has managed to find its way onto countless blogs around the world. Here is a link to the image as posted on my blog june3rd.com/boat.

2. Weston, D., Blagov, P. S., Harenski, K., Kilts, C., & Hamann, S. (2006). Neural bases of motivated reasoning: An fmri study of emotional constraints on partisan political judgment in the 2004 U.S. presidential election. *Journal of Cognitive Neuroscience*, 18 (11), 1947-1958. doi:10.1162/jocn.2006.18.11.1947

3. Weston's findings were presented at the 2006 Annual Conference of the Society for Personality and Social Psychology and reported through varies media outlets (including www.nbcnews.com/id/11009379/ns/technology_an d_science-science/t/political-bias-affects-brain-activity-study-finds) and is the basis for Weston's 2007/2008 book *The Political Brain: The Role of Emotion in Deciding the Fate of the Nation* (New York, NY: Public Affairs).

Chapter 10

1. Twain, M. as quoted in Parrott, L. (2000). *The control freak: Coping with those around you. Taming the one within.* Wheaton, IL. Tyndale.
2. Attributed to Albert Einstein (1879-1955).
3. Gray, J. (1993). *Men are from Mars, women are from Venus: A practical guide for improving communication and getting what you want in your relationships.* New York, NY: Harper Collins.
4. Carothers, B. J., & Reis, H. T. (2012). Men and women are from Earth: Examining the latent structure of gender. *Journal of Personality and Social Psychology.* 104 (2), 385-407. doi:10.1037/a0030437
5. Lee, T. L. (2012). *Good idea. now what: How to move from idea to execution.* Hoboken, NJ. Wiley.

Chapter 11

1. Plato (trans 1888). *The Republic of Plato* (3rd ed.). B. Jowett (Trans). Oxford: Clarendon Press.
2. Thoreau H. D. (1993). *A year in Thoreau's journal, 1851.* New York, NY: Penguin.
3. Leonard, G. (1991). *Mastery: The keys to success and long-term fulfillment.* St. Paul, MN. Penguin.

Chapter 12

1. Karampatsos, J. M. (2012). A marriage between two perceptions: How spirituality and perceived similarity between husbands and wives impacts marital satisfaction (Order No. 3501335). Available from ProQuest Dissertations & Theses Full Text. (929136522).

2. **Religious Commitment Inventory-10 (RCI-10).** Worthington (1988) proposed a model that theorized highly religiously committed people tended to evaluate their world on religious dimensions based on their religious values, and developed the RCI to measure the degree to which individuals adhere to their religious values, beliefs, and practices. **Faith Maturity Scale (FMS).** Developed by Benson, Donahue, and Erickson (1993), the FMS was designed to assess "the degree to which a person embodies the priorities, commitments, and perspectives characteristic of vibrant and life-transforming faith" (p. 3). A twelve-item short form has also been developed with the authors reporting internal consistency reliability of .88 and correlation with the long form of .94 and was used in this study. **Mini-International Personality Item Pool (Mini-IPIP).** Donellen, Oswald, Baird and Lucas (2006) developed the 20-item Mini-IPIP as a short form to the 50-item International Personality Item Pool— Five-Factor Model measure (IPIP-FFM, Goldberg, 1999) to be used as a very short measure of the Big Five personality traits. As measured by the Mini-IPIP, the Big Five dimensions of personality are Extraversion, a measure of propensity to experience positive emotions and to seek stimulation and the company of others; Agreeableness, a measure of tendency to be compassionate and cooperative;

Conscientiousness, a measure of goal-directed behavior and amount of control over impulses; Neuroticism, a measure of affect and emotional control; and Intellect/Imagination—also referred to as Openness or Openness to Experience in other FFM measures, measure of the scope of imagination, urge for experiences, artistic interest, and independent mindedness. **PREPARE/ENRICH.** Olson, Larson and Olson (2009) developed the PREPARE/ENRICH inventory to measure the strength and growth areas in couples at various stages in a relationship in order to assist clergy and clinicians provide relationship counseling. A 30-item assessment comprising of three 10-item subscales (satisfaction, communication, conflict resolution) has been made available specifically for researchers and will be used in this study. **Demographic Questionnaire.** A demographic questionnaire accompanied the measures to collect information such as (a) length of marriage, (b) number of previous marriages, (c) marital status of parents, (d) level of income, (e) ethnicity, (f) age, (g) gender, (h) religious affiliation, (i) frequency of prayer, (j) frequency of religious service attendance, and (k) number of children.

3. Wise, R. (Producer & Director). (1965) The sound of music. (Motion Picture). United States. 20th Century Fox.

Chapter 13

1. Felice Varini's official website can be found at www.varini.org. If you do not speak French you can have the website translated or visit Wikipedia® for some sample images and additional links: en.wikipedia.org/wiki/Felice_Varini

2. The $64,000 Question was an American TV game show aired on CBS from 1955-1958. As with the CBS radio quiz show Take It or Leave It (1940-1947)—whose top prize was awarded for answering "The $64 Question" correctly—and several spin-offs and copycats throughout the years, contestants are asked a series of increasingly difficult questions with the potential cash prize increasing.
3. Millar, M. (1942). *The weak-eyed bat*. Garden City, NY: Doubleday.
4. Thoreau, H. D. (1849). *A week on the Concord and Merrimack rivers*. Boston, MA: James Munroe and Company.
5. Attributed to Robert McCloskey (1914-2003).
6. Framo, J. (1982). *Explorations in marital & family therapy: Selected papers of James L. Framo*. New York, NY: Springer Publishing Company.

Chapter 14

1. This quote was in a letter to a friend in 1840 and appears in reprinted works such as: Emerson, R. W. (2011). *Selected writings of Ralph Waldo Emerson*. New York, NY: Penguin.
2. Walters, L. (1993). *Secrets of successful speakers: How you can motivate, captivate and persuade*. New York, NY: McGraw-Hill.
3. Detz, J. (2000). *It's not what you say, it's how you say* it. New York, NY: St. Martin's Griffen.
4. Attributed to Mohandas Karamchand Gandhi (1869-1948).
5. Gordon, T. (2001). *Leader effectiveness training L. E. T.: Proven skills for leading today's business into tomorrow*. New York, NY: Berkley Publishing Group.
6. Bloom, A. (1970). *Beginning to pray*. New York: Paulist Press.

7. Bridges, J. (1994). *The discipline of grace: God's role and our role in the pursuit of holiness.* Colorado Springs, CO: NavPress.
8. Attributed to Chief Justice and former Secretary of State John Marshall (1755-1835).

Chapter 15

1. Lewis, C. S. (1943). *The case for Christianity.* New York: Macmillan.
2. The origins of this question can be traced as far back as at least 1710 to philosopher George Berkeley book *A Treatise Concerning the Principles of Human Knowledge* in the question, ""But, say you, surely there is nothing easier than for me to imagine trees, for instance, in a park [...] and nobody by to perceive them." For further reading on the evolution of this question see en.wikipedia.org/wiki/If_a_tree_falls_in_a_forest.
3. Gordon, T. (2001). *Leader effectiveness training L. E. T.: Proven skills for leading today's business into tomorrow.* New York, NY: Berkley Publishing Group.

Chapter 16

1. Kendrick, S. & Kendrick, A. (2008). *The love dare.* Nashville, TN: B&H Publishing Group.
2. Attributed to Mohandas Karamchand Gandhi (1869-1948), but the quote is believed to be derivation of something Gandhi did say, *"If we could change ourselves, the tendencies in the world would also change. As a man changes his own nature, so does the attitude of the world change towards him. This is the divine mystery supreme. A wonderful thing it is and the source of our happiness. We need not wait to see what others do."* (Quoted from *Collected Works of Mahatma Gandhi*

(1964) Publications Division, Ministry of Information and Broadcasting, Government of India).

3. Covey, S. (1989). *The 7 habits of highly effective people: Powerful lessons in personal change.* New York: Simon & Schuster.

4. Loy, R. (2011). *3 questions: A powerful grid to help you live by the grace of God.* Springfield, MO: Influence Resources.

5. Attributed to St. Augustine of Hippo (354-430).

6. For more information on the research of John Gottman visit www.gottman.com/research.

7. Batterson, M. (2011). *The circle maker: Praying circles around your biggest dreams and greatest fears.* Grand Rapids, MD: Zondervan.

8. The original quote attributed to Frederick Douglas is "One and God make a majority" as quoted in Tryon Edwards' *A Dictionary of Thoughts: Being a Cyclopedia of Laconic Quotations from the Best Authors of the World, Both Ancient and Modern* (1906). Detroit, MI: F.B. Dickerson Company. Frederick Douglas is also said to have stated, "One with God is a majority" and "The man who is right is a majority" according to *Frederick Douglass: The colored orator* by Frederic May Holland, 1969, Haskell House. Thomas Reed is quoted as having said "One, with God, is always a majority, but many a martyr has been burned at the stake while the votes were being counted."

Chapter 17

1. The Nobel Memorial Prize in Economics Sciences was awarded in 1994 to John C. Harsanyi, John F. Nash Jr., and Reinhard Selten for "their pioneering analysis of equilibria in the theory of non-cooperative games."

2. Goff, B. (2012). *Love does: Discover a secretly incredible life in an ordinary world.* Nashville, TN: Thomas Nelson.

3. Lencioni, P. (2002). *The five dysfunctions of a team: A leadership fable.* San Fransisco, CA: Jossey-Bass.

4. This quote is an excerpt from President Richard Milhous Nixon's 1st Inaugural Address given on January 20, 1969 from the East Front of the United States Capitol and televised via satellite around the world.

5. Lewis, C. S. (1952). *Mere Christianity.* New York, NY. Macmillan.

6. Lewis, C. S. (1949). On Forgiveness. In *The Weight of Glory: And Other Addresses.* New York, NY: HarperCollins.

Chapter 18

1. Olson, Larson and Olson developed the PREPARE/ENRICH inventory to measure the strength and growth areas in couples at various stages in a relationship in order to assist clergy and clinicians provide relationship counseling. Over the past 30 years over 3 million couples have used the assessment. More information is available at www.prepare-enrich.com.

2. Kendrick, S. & Kendrick, A. (2008). *The love dare.* Nashville, TN: B&H Publishing Group.

3. The ancient military treatise *The Art of War* was written by a high ranking Chinese military general, Sun Tzu, and translated into English by Lionel Giles in 1910.

4. Framo, J. (1982). *Explorations in marital & family therapy: Selected papers of James L. Framo.* New York, NY: Springer Publishing Company.

5. Chapman, G. (1992). *The five love languages: How to express heartfelt commitment to your mate.* Chicago, IL: Northfield Publishing.

Chapter 19

1. Lewis, C. S. (1955). *The Magician's Nephew.* London: Bodley Head.
2. While the majority of the world may believe the Earth is round, there are still those who believe the Earth is flat and have some surprisingly convincing science to back up their claims. The Flat Earth Society's (theflatearthsociety.org) mission statements says, "The mission of the Flat Earth Society is to promote and initiate discussion of Flat Earth theory as well as archive Flat Earth literature. Our forums act as a venue to encourage free thinking and debate." For a fascinating and informative video explanation of flat Earth theories check out Michael Steven's Vsauce posting from December 4, 2014: youtube.com/watch?v=VNqNnUJVcVs
3. Starr, C. (1969). Social benefit versus technological risk. *Science,* 165, 1232-1238. doi:10.1126/science.165.3899.1232
4. Wald, A. (1943) A method of estimating plane vulnerability based on damage of survivors. Statistical Research Group, Columbia University. cna.org/sites/default/files/research/0204320000.pdf
5. Mangel, M. & Samaniego, F. (1984). Abraham Wald's work on aircraft survivability". *Journal of the American Statistical Association,* 79 (386), 259–267. doi:10.2307/2288257
6. Stanley, A. (2004). *Louder than words: The power of uncompromised living.* Sisters, OR: Multnomah.

What People are Saying About
The Elephant in the Marriage
and Dr Jason Karampatsos

Dr. Karampatsos has a passionate heart to see marriages thrive within God's design. He challenged my wife and I to examine our perspectives in order to let go of eroding perceptions and work on strengthening communication. Few others have spoken life into our marriage as poignantly as Dr. Karampatsos.

-Daryl Alston

When Gilbert and I decided to take Pastor Jason's Marriage 101 class, I anticipated specific takeaways. Most important, while I felt I could not have what he and his wife had, I wanted to be able to feel it through their interaction, which for me, would help authenticate what we would learn.
When I sat in the class on the first night I observed them and it made me feel we made the right choice. We especially enjoyed the discussions on communication as these helped us see where we were going wrong. I was excited to put into action what I was learning, and was ecstatic when my husband started incorporating what he learned when communicating. In addition, role playing different scenarios served as real eye openers and I had several "light bulb" moments.
This class was indeed pivotal to the positive turn in our marriage and we are fortunate it was offered when we really needed help. I would refer others to his class, and would definitely buy his book.

-Jackielyn and Gilbert Guyah

Dr. Jason's book allowed us to procure a more in-depth understanding of marriage from a godly perspective. It empowered us with practical, yet powerful tools that could easily be applied to our daily lives, which greatly strengthened the love, respect, and communication in our relationship with each other, as well as our spiritual growth with God. Dr. Jason has captured God's original intent for what a marriage should look like and has articulated these lessons in a way that can be easily understood and applied by married couples in every stage of their marriage. Dr. Jason's lessons illustrate that applying God's principles for marriage and communication are the key ingredients to strengthening and sustaining any marriage. We highly recommend Dr. Jason's book and the godly lessons that it presents to any married couple new or old.

-Sandy and Corey Jones

My spouse and I attended two marriage courses led by Dr. Karampatsos and his wife, Jennifer, implementing many techniques offered in his book, The Elephant in the Marriage. The practical examples outlined in his book applied to class members from various learning styles, cultures, and experiences allowing everyone to relate and learn. Using examples outlined in his book, combined with years of pastoral, academic, and clinical counseling experience, Dr. Karampatsos was able to help class participants examine and understand the relationship between life experiences and expectations/perspectives, and identify healthier viewpoints/approaches that would strengthen their marriages. I highly recommend this book as it allowed my spouse and me to identify hidden areas of conflict, and it fostered a desire to go deeper in our relationship.

–Wife, and mother of two

My wife and I attended the six week session of Marriage 101 taught by Dr. Jason Karampatsos and his wife, Jennifer. The material covered every aspect of marriage, allowing us to leave having identified strength and growth areas. Our takeaway for growth was that perception is your reality; we now communicate better so that our reality is not a misguided perception. The teaching by Dr. Jason also helped us recognize a strength in our marriage is that in most areas we are unified. This gives us encouragement and gratitude that a marriage based on Christian principles is not only attainable, but with love and prayer, it will withstand the attacks sure to come. Dr. Jason's book will breathe life into a dying marriage and give a wakeup call to a stale one!

-Craig Vance

Dr. Jason was truly a blessing for my wife and me. He poured his heart and soul into listening to us and then providing us with practical, unbiased biblical principles to help heal–first as individuals, and then as a couple joined together as one. He helped us both to take introspective looks at ourselves and to see things from a perspective other than our own. We can't thank him enough for his genuine, biblically inspired marriage ministry.

-Erik and Leah Johnson

ABOUT THE AUTHOR

Dr. Jason Karampatsos is the lead pastor of New Life Assembly of God in Janesville, Wisconsin and the co-founder of the City of Refuge Counseling Network. As an ordained minister and a licensed counselor with a Ph.D. in pastoral counseling, he has been able to help men, women, families, pastors, and churches navigate spiritual and mental health challenges.

He writes extensively on the impact of perspectives and perceptions upon everyday realities and especially upon marriages addressing relationship issues from a Christian perspective. He is an active speaker for marriage retreats and workshops, and speaks to pastors and churches across the country on how to have healthy relationships in the church and in ministry.

Dr. Karampatsos and his wife, Jennifer, have been married for over 20 years. While raising three children of their own, both have worked to help thousands of couples across the country realize that God not only wants them to survive their relationships, but to thrive.

To learn more, or schedule him to speak, follow his blog or find more information at **www.june3rd.com**.

Made in the USA
Monee, IL
05 February 2020

21343489R00143